# Standardized Method of Life Cycle Costing for Construction Procurement

# Standardized Method of Life Cycle Costing for Construction Procurement

A supplement to BS ISO 15686-5:2008 Buildings and constructed assets – Service life planning – Part 5: Life cycle costing

BCIS

BSi Business Information

First published in the UK in 2008

by
BSI
389 Chiswick High Road
London W4 4AL



Typeset in Helvetica Neue by Monolith – http://www.monolith.uk.com
Printed in Great Britain by The MFK Group, Stevenage

*British Library Cataloguing in Publication Data*
A catalogue record for this book is available from the British Library

ISBN 978-0-580-62662-3

# FOREWORD

## Publishing Information

This Published Document provides practical guidance on the application in the UK of BS ISO 15686-5. It is published by BSI and came into effect on 30 June 2008. It was prepared by BSI Technical Subcommittee B/500/3, Durability.

## Acknowledgements

The committee wishes to acknowledge the particular contribution of the following members in leading the development of this document:

| | |
|---|---|
| Joe Martin | BCIS, Executive Director of Building Cost Information Service |
| Andrew Green | Faithful+Gould, Director and Head of Whole Life Value Consultancy |
| Kathryn Bourke | Faithful+Gould, Convenor of ISO TC 59/SC 14/WG14, responsible for the development of ISO 15686-5: *Life cycle costing* |

The drafting was assisted by a collaborative working group comprising:

| | |
|---|---|
| Hywel Davies | Chartered Institution of Building Services Engineers (CIBSE), Technical Director, and Chairman of B/500/3 |
| Ed Bartlett | Balfour Beatty Capital |
| Charles Whitlock | BSI |
| Paul Wornell | Building LifePlans |
| Peter Mayer | Building LifePlans |
| Mike Clift | BRE |
| Peter Cunningham | Constructing Excellence |
| Paul Frances | Defence Estates |
| Adrian Wilkins | Faithful+Gould |
| Phil Heenan | OGC, Policy Team Leader of Smarter Construction |

In the course of its preparation, this document underwent wider consultation amongst practitioners, clients and industry subject experts. Amongst those organizations consulted were:

BSI Consumer and Public Interest Network
Chartered Institution of Building
Construction Confederation
Construction Products Association
Department of Communities and Local Government
Fibre and Cement Manufacturers' Association
Home Office
Institution of Structural Engineers
Scottish QS Faculty Board
Royal Institution of Chartered Surveyors (RICS) Quantity Surveyor's Measurement group

and the following companies and practices:

Bovis Lend Lease
Vita Lend Lease

Carillion
Cyril Sweett
Davis Langdon LLP
E C Harris
Faithful+Gould
Gardiner and Theobald
Gleeds
Operon
Rider Levett Bucknall
Skanska
Turner and Townsend
Whole Life Consultants Ltd

The committee particularly wishes to acknowledge the contribution made by the late Dr D P Wyatt, who as an active member for many years contributed significantly to the development of this document and of BS ISO 15686-5.

## Use of this document

The context of this document, and, in particular, its relationship with BS ISO 15686-5, is discussed in the Introduction.

As a guide, this Published Document takes the form of guidance and recommendations. It should not be quoted as if it were a specification and particular care should be taken to ensure that claims of compliance are not misleading.

It has been assumed in the preparation of this Published Document that the execution of its provisions will be entrusted to appropriately qualified and experienced people, for whose use it has been produced.

## Contractual and legal considerations

This publication does not purport to include all the necessary provisions of a contract. Users are responsible for its correct application.

**This Published Document is not to be regarded as a British Standard.**

# CONTENTS

# INTRODUCTION 1

## What is life cycle costing?

1.1 The definitions of life cycle costing used in this document are from the International Standard BS ISO 15686-5: Life cycle Costing. Key definitions include:

> ***Life cycle cost (LCC) is 'cost of an asset, or its parts throughout its life cycle, while fulfilling the performance requirements'.***
>
> *(BS ISO 15686-5, 3.1.1.7)*
>
> ***Life cycle costing is 'methodology for the systematic economic evaluation of life cycle costs over a period of analysis, as defined in the agreed scope'.***
>
> Note: life cycle costing can address a period of analysis which covers the entire life cycle, or selected stage(s) or periods of interest therein.
>
> *(BS ISO 15686-5, 3.1.1.8).*

1.2 There are also some references to whole life costing, which has a broader scope than life cycle costing: (Refer to Annex A for a menu of the cost headings included in whole life costing and life cycle costing.)

> ***Whole life costing is 'methodology for the systematic economic consideration of all whole life costs and benefits over a period of analysis, as defined in the agreed scope'.***
>
> Note: the projected costs or benefits may include finance, business costs, income from land sale, user costs.
>
> *(BS ISO 15686-5, 3.1.1.15)*

**The objectives of the Standardized Method for Life Cycle Costing (SMLCC) for Construction Procurement are to provide:**

1. A UK standard cost data structure for life cycle costing, which aligns with BS ISO 15686-5 and with the BCIS Standard Form of Capital Cost Analysis (SFCA) and industry recognized occupancy cost codes. (Refer to Annex A, B and C)
2. Life cycle costing practitioners with a standardized method of applying life cycle costing, applicable to the UK construction industry and to the key stages of the procurement process.
3. Process mapping the life cycle costing stages – to help structure how to plan, generate, interpret and present the results for a variety of different purposes and levels of life cycle cost planning.
4. Instructions on how to define the client's specific requirements for life cycle costing and the required outputs and forms of reporting – and to decide on which method of economic evaluation to apply.
5. Simplification and demystification – by providing practical guidance, instructions and definitions, together with informative worked examples on how to undertake life cycle costing (for construction).
6. An industry accepted methodology, to facilitate a more accurate, consistent and robust application of life cycle costing estimation and option appraisals – thereby creating a more effective and robust basis for life cycle cost analysis and benchmarking.

> This document also seeks to help eliminate confusion over scoping and terminology and to address concerns over the uncertainty and risks that are undermining confidence in life cycle costs used for construction procurement.

## What is BS ISO 15686, and why does it need a supplement?

1.3 BS ISO 15686 is a multi-part series of international standards giving guidance on various aspects of planning the service life of buildings and constructed assets. It has a wide audience of users, covering all those involved in procuring, designing, constructing and managing, or owning and running buildings. Part 5 covers life cycle costing. It provides guidelines, definitions, principles and informative text on the application of life cycle costing techniques in the context of service-life planning. It also covers some aspects of whole life costing and investment appraisal. It describes links to other aspects of guidance in the rest of the BS ISO 15686 series, such as how cost and environmental appraisal can be used to improve the sustainability of building constructed assets (notably energy performance and carbon emissions). However, it does not cover specific national issues, such as UK cost data conventions and other key aspects, which will be covered by this publication.

## Who needs this standardized methodology?

1.4 Construction consultants, their professional associations and construction procurement clients and funders jointly need an industry-accepted methodology on how to define the specific briefing requirements and then undertake life cycle costing. By standardizing the application of life cycle costing, in practice it can become more widely used across all forms of private- and public-sector construction procurement. The primary users of this document are expected to be life cycle costing practitioners and clients who commission life cycle costing and also building owners and facilities managers.

## Who produced this publication?

1.5 This guide was the result of cross-construction-industry collaboration and was produced by a technical drafting team and consultative working group. It is a supplement to BS ISO 15686-5: 2008 Buildings and constructed assets – Service life planning – Life cycle costing. It is hereafter referred to as the *Standardized Method of Life Cycle Costing (SMLCC) for Construction Procurement*.

## When to undertake life cycle costing

1.6 Life cycle costing is relevant throughout the building or constructed asset's life cycle, in particular during the project planning, design and construction and also during the in-use phases. This publication focuses on the application of project life cycle costing for construction procurement. (See Figure 1.1.)

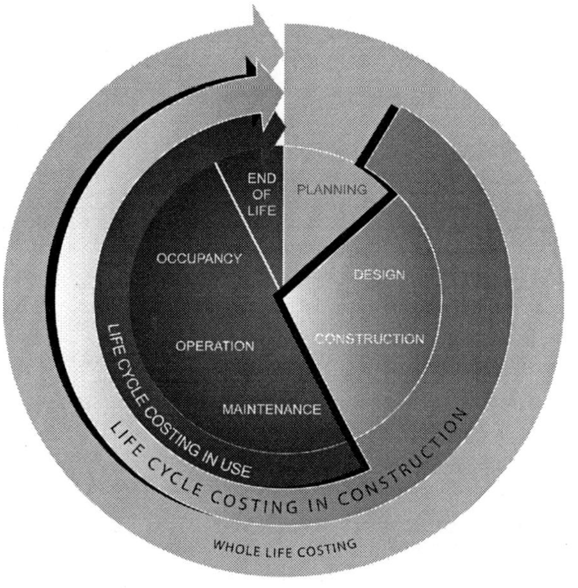


*Figure 1.1 Life cycle cost planning at different stages during a building or constructed asset's lifespan.*

*(adapted from BS ISO 15686-5, figure 4)*

## How is life cycle costing typically used for construction procurement?

1.7 Life cycle costing is an economic evaluation method that takes account of all relevant costs over the defined time horizon (period of study), including adjusting for the time value of money (i.e. net present value [NPV], or internal rate of return, or payback period, if required). The two most common ways in which life cycle costing is used in the UK construction industry are:

1. to generate a cash flow prediction over a given period of time;
2. to undertake an option appraisal study, in order to evaluate various solutions to a given design and construction problem.

1.8 Cash flow predictions are commonly used in public- and private-sector construction procurement to establish an expenditure profile (e.g. six-monthly or yearly, over the period of study) which can be used to set up a sinking fund for LCCs and also input into a wider economic evaluation (e.g. whole life costing). LCC cash flow predictions are also used as part of a budgeting process.

1.9 A prediction of a cash flow over a given period of time may be generated for a single asset (e.g. a boiler) or for a multiple of assets (e.g. an air-conditioning system, or a whole building level).

1.10 An option appraisal may use the cash flows of multiple solutions to a problem in order to compare the results – with or without a 'base case' (e.g. in Private Finance Initiative [PFI] construction procurement, the base case would be a public-sector comparator; for a component study, the base case could be one type of boiler).

1.11 LCC planning of a cash flow or option appraisals can be undertaken at different stages and levels of study, as broadly defined in item 2.9 and items 4.5 and 4.7.

## Life cycle costing may be part of a wider economic project evaluation

1.12 Life cycle costing may well form part of a wider economic project evaluation, which considers:

- whole life costs (including non-construction costs such as finance, business costs and also income from sales and disposals etc.);
- whole life value; best value;
- economically most advantageous tenders (EMAT).

Alternatively, it may feed into a project financial or economic investment appraisal or into a business case.

1.13 Life cycle costing may also be considered as part of an environmental or sustainability assessment.

## What costs to include/exclude and how to express them

1.14 Section 3 of this publication identifies what costs can be included or excluded and how to express them. This includes clarifying the differences between whole life costs (WLC) and LCC. Section 3 also provides a common cost breakdown structure and definitions for the UK construction industry.

1.15 Cost data are available from various historical and industry sources such as the BCIS Building Running Costs On Line Service, the International Occupiers Property Databank (OPD) or clients' and consultants' cost databases. Some costs, such as energy, may come from a predictive calculation.

1.16 Cost data from buildings in use and from manufacturers are available but should be used with caution.

1.17 This standardized method of life cycle costing provides a common cost breakdown structure for the UK construction industry, which should help to overcome the confusion over terminology and thereby significantly improve the confidence and robustness of LCC predictions and analysis of future construction projects.

# GUIDING PRINCIPLES 2

## The process of life cycle costing

2.1 The main steps in the process of life cycle costing are:

- define carefully the purpose and scope of the life cycle costing;
- plan the procedure;
- establish the rules and methodology to be applied;
- compile the available information and record the data assumptions;
- undertake the calculations and validate the results;
- apply risk and sensitivity analysis;
- interpret the results carefully;
- report the results and document all the information and assumptions used;
- review the report with the client and obtain agreement to the final outputs;
- do an LCC analysis for comparative benchmarking purposes (optional);
- release a final authorized and signed copy of the life cycle costing report.

2.2 Iterations of the process may be required, and the level of detail and form of analysis and reporting will change over the period of the construction project's procurement life cycle.

## Agreeing the brief for life cycle costing

2.3 The key requirements in formalizing the brief for life cycle costing are:

- agree the purpose;
- agree the precise scope of costs to be included and excluded and how to express them (using the standard menu of costs included in Annex A);
- agree the period of analysis and the method of economic evaluation;
- agree the level of detail of the LCC plan;
- establish the specific study inputs and rules (such as: base dates, units of costs and time, discount or inflation rates; indexation for location and tender price adjustment – base build elements; the extent of risks and uncertainty and other sensitivity analysis that is to be applied);
- confirm whether there is a standard project benchmark or base case to use as a comparator.

2.4 The brief will need to be tailored to the client's specific project requirements. In some cases, the life cycle costing practitioner may need to propose a basis for the LCC planning, particularly to clients unfamiliar with life cycle costing. Certain factors may significantly affect the outcomes. It is therefore important to understand the implications of applying certain factors (such as the period of analysis, or the discount rate used) and to make sure these are properly considered at the outset.

## Undertaking life cycle costing and analyzing the results

2.5 Life cycle costing is a systematic economic evaluation method used to establish an expenditure profile over the period of study. It comprises the following key elements:

- costing of predicted events or activities (to the applicable scope of costs and level of detail);
- timing of the predicted events or activities;

- analysis of the results (i.e. challenging and validating the outputs against the project brief);
- applying factoring methods and sensitivity analysis to the results (as defined in Section 6).

2.6 Life cycle costing may feed into a project economic investment and or project option appraisal, which may also draw on techniques such as environmental assessment, risk assessment modelling and benefit assessment. All of these techniques share the same basic principles that they should be objective, evidence based and performed at an appropriate level of detail, as agreed in the project-scoping brief.

2.7 LCC planning can be used to compare different design solutions with different cash flows, with or without having a base case (e.g. comparing alternative cladding forms with a brick and block work cavity wall construction).

2.8 The level of study will depend on the stage of project procurement and the available data to input.

2.9 An LCC plan may cover a single asset or multiple assets. Possible levels of study are:

- multiple assets or portfolio/estate level;
- single asset or whole building level;
- cluster level (multiple element, e.g. all windows and doors);
- element level (e.g. a roof);
- system level (e.g. an air-conditioning system);
- component or sub-component level (e.g. a boiler).

*Refer to the worked examples included in Annex D, which illustrate how to undertake a life cycle costing at a whole building level and also at a system and component detailed level.*

2.10 The most appropriate available data sources should be used. These may be in the public domain or not, but the origin should be recorded. Refer to Section 7.

2.11 Identify the relevant risks and uncertainty and agree the mitigation and sensitivity analysis to be applied.

*Refer to Section 6 and the example of an LCC risk log included in Annex E.*

## LCC reporting and producing the required outputs

2.12 Define the reporting and form of the required outputs in the scoping of the client's particular brief, including what will be the specific use of the outputs and precise cost-breakdown requirements. In addition, agree how the life cycle costing calculations will be checked and validated and then reported, reviewed and sanctioned by the client.

*(See Section 4, which describes the typical uses of the LCC plan and outputs required for specific purposes, including discounting of future costs and dealing with end of life cost.)*

2.13 Reporting of the LCC plan may be at a lesser level of detail than the underlying analysis. For example, analysis may be at elemental level, whereas reporting may be at whole-building level.

2.14 Life cycle costing has many variables, so it is important to record the purpose, scope and the form and level of economic evaluation and also all the underlying assumptions, information and data sources used. See Section 7 for general guidance and instructions.

2.15 The limitations of the LCC plan and known interfaces with other reports should be reported.

2.16 Retain the records and/or original data sources for an appropriate period of time after completion of the LCC plan and the final report.

2.17 It is important to understand what costs (and incomes, if applicable) are included in the LCC plan, to avoid omissions or double counting.

2.18 This publication provides a standard form for LCC analysis, in Annex F, to help structure capturing project LCCs for use in future cost planning and benchmarking studies. This form should be used in practice to enable and inform the accuracy of comparative LCC analysis, including highlighting any customization or specific divergence in the client's project brief.

# LIFE CYCLE COST DATA 3

# STRUCTURE AND DEFINITIONS

## What costs to include or exclude and how to express them

3.1 Agreement should be reached as to the precise scope of what relevant costs are to be included or excluded and how to express them before attempting to undertake a life cycle costing study.

3.2 This section provides a UK cost data structure for life cycle costing and clarifies which costs are part of the whole life cost (WLC) and which should normally be included under the major cost headings for LCC as shown in Figure 3.1.

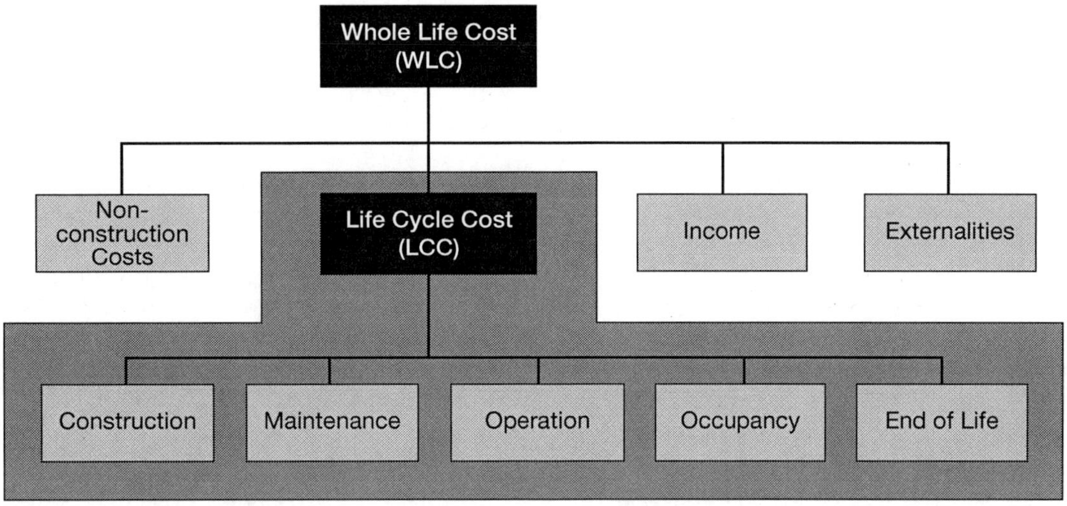


*Figure 3.1 Illustrating the difference between whole life cost (WLC) and life cycle cost (LCC).*

(adapted from BS ISO 15686-5, figure 2)

3.3 Figure 3.1 is based on the BS ISO 15686-5 standard cost breakdown structure and menu of costs.

3.4 Occupancy costs are included in BS ISO 15686-5 as part of the non-construction costs, but it is common practice in the UK to include relevant occupancy costs within the LCC.

3.5 Major repairs and replacement costs are commonly known as the 'life cycle replacement costs', excluding the annual planned preventative maintenance, minor repairs and unscheduled maintenance.

3.6 This publication provides a standardized method for life cycle costing based on linking the capital costs convention in BCIS Standard Form of Cost Analysis format (which may be for a new build, major capital investment or refurbishment of an existing constructed asset) to the generation of the LCC plan.

*(See Annex C, which maps how the UK construction industry accepted capital costs categories link to life cycle costing and to the total occupancy cost conventions using the BCIS standard form of cost analysis elemental cost categories and the International Total Occupancy Cost [ITOC] codes.)*

## UK LCC data structure and definitions

3.7 The standard cost breakdown for life cycle costing, for UK construction procurement, is provided in Table 3.1.

*Table 3.1 UK LCC data structure and definitions*

| Item | Life Cycle Cost Category | Definitions |
|---|---|---|
| **1.0** | **Construction costs** | Costs payable by the client, for and in connection with the initial new building works and/or refurbishment works. |
| **1.1** | **Construction works costs** | Cost of initial construction of the building and external works. Presented in the BCIS Standard Form of Cost Analysis (SFCA) format – adopting the elemental cost structure and coding:<br><br>1. Substructure<br>2. Superstructure<br>3. Finishes<br>4. Fittings<br>5. Services<br>6. External works<br>7. Preliminaries<br>8. Contingency (including risk allowances)<br>9. Contractor's design fees. |
| **1.2** | **Other construction related costs**<br><br>*Note – Excluded from the life cycle costing of maintenance activities, but could be included in the overall life cycle costing study* | Costs in connection with the initial construction. For example:<br><br>• Design related consultancy fees<br>• Special client costs – e.g. launch events and associated marketing costs<br>• Decanting (when not in the preliminaries)<br>• Infrastructure charges<br>• Infrastructure adoption and maintenance costs<br>• Highway costs<br>• Utility charges<br>• Licenses and permits<br>• Planning application/permission fees and building regulation fees<br>• Planning gain and other community financial contributions<br>• Party wall costs<br>• Rights to light costs<br>• Client's design development and project risk register contingency, i.e. risk allowances (if not included to 1.1). |
| **1.3** | **Client definable costs** | Other construction related costs that the client wants to include in the life cycle cost plan. For example for schools projects abnormals and enhancements are costed separately. |

| Item | Life Cycle Cost Category | Definitions |
|---|---|---|
| *Note 1 – Construction works should be presented as the BCIS Standard Form of Cost Analysis (SFCA) elements and sub-elements for buildings and external works.*<br>*Note 2 – Where separate enabling works contracts are included in the construction costs they should be shown separately in 1.2. Enabling works are defined as works required to allow the construction works to proceed, but have no future life cycle costs to the client, e.g. land remediation. Otherwise include in 6.1 whole life costs.*<br>*Note 3 – Construction costs for works or furniture, fittings and equipment (FF&E) that will not be maintained by the client, which will not therefore contribute to ongoing liabilities for life cycle costing, should be shown separately. For example roads to be adopted or equipment maintained/replaced by the occupier or user.*<br>*Note 4 – The initial costs of items forming part of occupancy costs, such as information and communication technology (ICT) or unfixed furniture, fittings and equipment (FF&E) should be shown separately.*<br>*Note 5 – Refer to Section 5 'Metrics' for guidance on presenting and comparing the costs.*<br>*Note 6 – Value added tax (VAT) is normally excluded (but if it is included, it must be stated separately).* | | |
| 2.0 | Maintenance costs | |
| **2.1** | **Major replacement costs** | Scheduled replacement of major systems and components. This will form the detailed asset life cycle replacement cost programme. |
| **2.2** | **Subsequent refurbishment and adaptation costs** | Scheduled refurbishment and adaptation during the period of analysis.<br><br>Exclude refurbishment and adaptation carried out as part of the initial construction, which should be included under the construction costs in 1.1. |
| **2.3** | **Redecorations** | Scheduled redecorations. Excludes redecorations carried out in connection with 2.1, 2.2, 2.4 and 2.5. |
| **2.4** | **Minor replacement, repairs and maintenance costs** | Scheduled replacement of parts and scheduled maintenance and repairs to components and associated making good and minor redecorations including planned preventative and/or reliability centred maintenance. |
| **2.5** | **Unscheduled replacement, repairs and maintenance costs** | Allowance for unforeseen or unplanned maintenance arising from early failure, inappropriate use etc. |
| **2.6** | **Grounds maintenance** | Where it is costed separately (e.g. tree replacement, lawn mowing and landscape maintenance). Note – normally grounds maintenance is included with the external works element. |
| **2.7** | **Client definable costs** | Other maintenance related costs that the client wants to include in the life cycle cost plan. |

| Item | Life Cycle Cost Category | Definitions |
|---|---|---|
| *Note 1 – Major replacement (2.1) and subsequent refurbishment (2.2) redecorations (2.3) should generally be shown in BCIS SFCA element and sub-element cost structure categories, for buildings and external works – as listed in item 1.1 above.*<br>*Note 2 – Minor replacement, repairs and maintenance costs (2.4) and unscheduled replacement, repairs and maintenance costs (2.5) and grounds maintenance (2.6) can be presented in an elemental cost structure, but are normally calculated as whole building costs. (Note – see the informative worked example Annex D).*<br>*Note 3 – The split between 'major' and 'minor' replacement will depend on the funding arrangements and contractual interface agreements, and should be defined on each project. For example, if a life cycle major replacement fund is set up, it may be defined by the life of the components or the cost of the replacement. It is recommended that the detailed splits by assets or sub-asset should be made transparent and recorded in an interface agreement.*<br>*Note 4 – Redecorations costs can be included within their associated elemental costings – e.g. they may be part of maintenance, costs, or in with other major LCC works sections – depending on the client specific requirements.*<br>*Note 5 – Include all costs or income from disposal of replaced components and parts, where applicable.*<br>*Note 6 – Include and show separately all overheads, associated temporary works, access costs, out of hours premium, design and commissioning costs etc., in connection with replacement, maintenance and repairs.*<br>*Note 7 – Include inspections (statutory and others) carried out as part of maintenance contract work. General inspections commissioned separately by or on behalf of the client should be included in '3.3 Administrative costs'.*<br>*Note 8 – Include costs for the contractor's management of the works and on- costs etc. – including any life cycle fund and management of the direct employed labour (DEL) where those costs are considered to be direct overheads to the work.*<br>*Note 9 – Refer to Section 5 'Metrics' for guidance on presenting and comparing the costs.*<br>*Note 10 – Value added tax (VAT) is normally excluded (but if it is included, it must be stated separately).* | | |
| **3.0** | **Operation costs** | Costs of operating the building and external works arising from the building itself rather than from its occupancy, excluding maintenance costs. |
| **3.1** | **Cleaning costs** | Cleaning costs include periodic, routine and specialist cleaning:<br><br>**3.1.1 Windows and external surfaces**<br><br>Cleaning windows, curtain walling, glazed screens, cladding, sun screening etc.<br><br>Exclude the cleaning of external wall surfaces accompanied by restoration (e.g. stonework); this should be included in 'Maintenance costs'. |

| Item | Life Cycle Cost Category | Definitions |
|---|---|---|
| 3.1 | Cleaning costs (continued) | **3.1.2 Internal cleaning**<br><br>Cleaning of internal surfaces. Includes;<br><br>• Cleaning floors, vacuum cleaning and shampooing carpets<br>• Cleaning internal surfaces of windows<br>• Cleaning internal wall surfaces<br>• Dusting and cleaning ledges, furniture and fittings<br>• Emptying waste bins<br>• Consumables to toilet facilities (e.g. paper towels, laundering roller towels, soap etc.)<br>• Other client definable items.<br><br>Excludes washing down walls or paintwork done in lieu of redecoration, which is included in 2.3 Redecorations.<br><br>**3.1.3 Specialist cleaning**<br><br>• Kitchen cleaning<br>• Atrium cleaning<br>• Other user definable items.<br><br>**3.1.4 External works cleaning**<br><br>• Cleaning of roads, paved areas etc.<br>• Cleaning street furniture<br>• Litter collection<br>• Emptying waste bins<br>• Snow clearing<br>• Graffiti removal<br>• Other client definable items. |
| 3.2 | Utilities costs | **3.2.1 Fuel**<br><br>Show cost of different fuels separately e.g.<br><br>• Gas<br>• Electricity<br>• Fuel oil<br>• Solid fuel (define)<br>• Other (e.g. wood chips for biomass boilers).<br><br>Include any income from renewable energy (e.g. income from selling energy back to the national grid, or generated for other usages).<br><br>Exclude cost of boiler men and such labour attending on mechanical and electrical equipment, which are included in '3.3 Administrative costs'. |

| Item | Life Cycle Cost Category | Definitions |
|---|---|---|
| 3.2 | **Utilities costs (continued)** | **3.2.2 Water and Drainage**<br><br>• Water rates<br>• Effluents, sewerage and drainage charges<br>• Others. |
| 3.3 | **Administrative costs** | User support costs related to the operation of the building and external works<br><br>**3.3.1 Property Management**<br><br>All costs involved in managing the operation and maintenance of the building.<br><br>Includes:<br><br>• Supervisory staffing e.g. building supervisor, maintenance manager, facilities managers etc<br>• Professional staff or consultants e.g. architects, engineers, surveyors<br>• Clerical staff and administrative staff<br>• General and regulatory surveys commissioned by or on behalf of the client.<br><br>Excludes:<br><br>• Contractors management of the works and of any life cycle fund and management of direct employed labour (DEL) whose costs are considered direct overheads to the work and should therefore be included in '2.0 Maintenance costs'<br>• Inspections, including statutory inspections, carried out as part of maintenance<br>• Dilapidation surveys and residual life surveys and inspections carried out in connection with disposal should be included in 5.1 Disposal inspections.<br>• Strategic asset management, estate agents fees etc.<br><br>**3.3.2 Staff engaged in servicing the building**<br><br>Contractors or directly employed staff attending upon the equipment directly serving the building. Including operatives partly responsible for maintenance and/or operation of equipment whose costs cannot be allocated to specific functions such as caretakers. |

| Item | Life Cycle Cost Category | Definitions |
|---|---|---|
| 3.3 | **Administrative costs (continued)** | Include:<br>• Labour attending upon the mechanical and electrical equipment<br>• Security staff for the building (i.e. operatives resource time)<br>• Toilet attendants<br>• Caretakers<br>• Consumables – materials and equipment required by staff engaged in servicing the building.<br><br>Exclude:<br>• Porters<br>• Reception.<br><br>**3.3.3 Waste management/disposal**<br><br>Contractors or directly employed staff engaged in the collection, compaction, removal and disposal and or recycling or waste from buildings or their grounds. Includes:<br><br>General waste<br><br>Toxic waste<br><br>Confidential waste<br><br>Sanitary waste<br><br>Recycling costs<br><br>Other client definable items. |
| 3.4 | **Overheads costs** | **Property insurance**<br>Premiums for insuring the property. |
| 3.5 | **Taxes (if applicable)** | **Rates and other local charges** payable in connection with owning the building. |
| 3.6 | **Client definable costs** | Other operation related costs that the client wants to include in the life cycle cost plan. |

| Item | Life Cycle Cost Category | Definitions |
|---|---|---|
| *Note 1 – Staff costs should include salaries, wages, expenses, overtime, insurances, administrative support, overheads, accommodation, supply of uniforms, travel costs, pensions etc.*<br>*Note 2 – Exclude costs that relate to the occupancy of the building such as laundry and bathroom consumables to hotel rooms.*<br>*Note 3 – Security, include the cost of staff, or contractors involved in providing security to the building. The cost of maintaining security equipment should be included in maintenance. The cost of staff or contractors involved in providing security in connection with the occupancy of the building should be included in occupancy costs.*<br>*Note 4 – Include and show separately all overheads, associated temporary works, access costs, out of hours premium, design and commissioning costs etc., in connection with operation costs.*<br>*Note 5 – Refer to Section 5 'Metrics' for guidance on presenting and comparing the costs.*<br>*Note 6 – Value added tax (VAT) is normally excluded (but if it is included, it must be stated separately).* | | |
| **4.0** | **Occupancy costs** | User support costs relating to the occupation of the building. |
| **4.1** | **Internal moves (churn)** | |
| **4.2** | **Reception and customer hosting** | |
| **4.3** | **Security** | Refer to operations and maintenance costs notes on security. |
| **4.4** | **Helpdesk** | |
| **4.5** | **Switchboard/telephones** | |
| **4.6** | **Post room – mail services/courier and external distribution services** | |
| **4.7** | **ICT and IT services** | |
| **4.8** | **Library services** | |
| **4.9** | **Catering and hospitality** | |
| **4.10** | **Laundry** | |
| **4.11** | **Vending** | |
| **4.12** | **Occupant's furniture, fittings and equipment (FF&E)** | May also include specialist equipment, such as medical equipment, equipment management etc. |
| **4.13** | **Internal plants and landscaping** | |
| **4.14** | **Stationery and reprographics** | |
| **4.15** | **Porters** | |

<table>
<tr><th>Item</th><th>Life Cycle Cost Category</th><th>Definitions</th></tr>
<tr><td>4.16</td><td>Car parking charges</td><td>Split into customer parking/staff and operational parking.</td></tr>
<tr><td>4.17</td><td>Client definable costs</td><td>Other occupancy costs that the client wants to include in the life cycle cost plan – e.g. business support costs such as:<br><br>• disaster recovery<br>• archiving<br>• transport costs<br>• other client definable items.</td></tr>
<tr><td colspan="3">Note 1 – Occupancy costs are classified in the BS ISO menu of costs as part of the 'non-construction costs' included under 'User support costs (3) Administration', and are therefore excluded from life cycle costing. In the UK clients may require that some of these costs form part of a life cycle cost study.<br>Note 2 – Where an initial investment is required, e.g. information and communication technology (ICT) services, or unfixed furniture, fittings and equipment (FF&E) the initial cost should be shown separately under 'Construction' in 1.1.<br>Note 3 – Include and show separately all overheads, associated temporary works, access costs, out of hours premium, design and commissioning costs etc., in connection with occupancy costs.<br>Note 4 – Refer to Section 5 'Metrics' for guidance on presenting and comparing the costs.<br>Note 5 – Value added tax (VAT) is normally excluded (but if it is included, it must be stated separately).</td></tr>
<tr><td>5.0</td><td>End of life costs</td><td>Costs payable and credits accruing at end of period of analysis.</td></tr>
<tr><td>5.1</td><td>Disposal inspections</td><td>Cost of inspections carried out in connection with demolition, dilapidations or other contractual requirements.</td></tr>
<tr><td>5.2</td><td>Demolition</td><td>Cost of demolition of the building at end of life or period of interest and landfill and recycling or disposal costs.</td></tr>
<tr><td>5.3</td><td>Reinstatement to meet the contractual requirements</td><td>Cost of dilapidations or for complying with other contractual obligations to return the building to a set standard of repair.</td></tr>
<tr><td>5.4</td><td>Client definable costs</td><td>Other end of life costs that the client wants to include in the life cycle cost costing.</td></tr>
<tr><td colspan="3">Note 1 – The 'end of life' for most life cycle costing calculations will be the end of the study period, and/or investment period, and not the end of life of the building.<br>Note 2 – Include and show separately all overheads, associated temporary works, access costs, out of hours premium, design and commissioning costs etc., in connection with end of life costs.<br>Note 3 – Refer to Section 5 – Metrics for guidance on presenting and comparing the costs<br>Note 4 – Value added tax (VAT) is normally excluded (but if it is included, it must be stated separately).</td></tr>
</table>

| Whole Life Cost Elements: these costs may be relevant, if LCC is part of a wider economic evaluation | | |
|---|---|---|
| | **Whole Life Cost Category** | Definitions |
| **6.0** | **Non-construction costs** | |
| **6.1** | **Land and enabling works** | Site costs (acquisition costs of the land and existing building). |
| **6.2** | **Finance costs** | Interest or cost of money and wider economic impact. |
| **6.3** | **Rental costs** | |
| **6.4** | **User support costs (1) – strategic estate management** | Includes in-house resources and real estate/ property management/general inspections, acquisition, disposal and removal. |
| **6.5** | **User support costs (2) – space charges** | PFI/PPP Service/Unitary charges, parking charges, charges for associated facilities. |
| **6.6** | **Taxes on costs** | Taxes on non-construction costs. |
| **6.7** | **User definable costs** | Other whole life costs that the user wants to include in the whole life cost plan. |
| *Note 1 – 'User support costs (3) Administration' is classified as 'Non-construction cost' in the BS ISO but has been included in the UK Supplement LCC structure as '4.0 Occupancy costs'* | | |
| **7.0** | **Income** | Income and other costs |
| **7.1** | **Income from sales** | Residual value on disposal of interest in land, constructed assets or salvaged materials, including grants etc. |
| **7.2** | **Third party income during occupation** | Rent and service charge payments PFI/PPP service/unitary payments. |
| **7.3** | **Taxes on income** | Taxes on land transactions and tax rebates (if applicable). |
| **Item** | **Whole Life Cost Category** | Definitions |
| **7.4** | **Loss of income** | Disruption, downtime loss of income and any relevant demands (e.g. contractual performance payment deductions). |
| **7.5** | **Client definable income** | Other income that the user wants to include in the whole life cost plan. |
| **8.0** | **Externalities** | Costs associated with the asset, which are not necessarily reflected in the transaction costs between provider and consumer. |
| **8.1** | | Client defined externalities to be included – if required. |

## Units of costs: real, nominal and discounted costs

3.8 In elemental LCC planning, the principal unit of costs for all elements of cost in scope shall be expressed in pounds sterling to two decimal places per square metre of gross internal floor area (GIFA).

3.9 In component LCC planning, the design and service-life performance criteria should be costed for against the systems, elements or components in scope. Special design and functional performance requirements shall be identified where applicable (e.g. energy usage and carbon-emissions targets).

3.10 Annual, periodic and cyclical costs are calculated at real costs (i.e. current prices with no allowance for inflation) within a cash flow over the required time period.

3.11 Nominal costs are expected costs at the date when the cost is due to be paid (e.g. technology replacement costs at the time when it is replaced or becomes obsolete).

3.12 The LCCs can be discounted and expressed as an NPV or some other form of economic valuation, such as internal rate of return (IRR) or payback period (PB).

*Guidance on how to do a discounted life cycle costing is provided in BS ISO 15686-5: Annex B.*

3.13 Lump sums and percentage adjustments shall be apportioned to the appropriate elements or cost categories.

3.14 Design fees and other consultancy fees, included in scope, should be stated for each element of the LCC plan, e.g. construction, maintenance, operation, occupancy and end of life.

3.15 Preliminaries, on costs, overheads and profit, out-of-hours working allowances, site preparation costs etc. should be shown separately, if required to be included in the scope of the life cycle costing.

3.16 Contingency should include the employer's contingency and any allowances for uncertainty and risks.

3.17 A list of costs specifically excluded from the life cycle costing should be stated, e.g. furniture, information and communications technology (ICT) etc.

## Glossary of cost definitions commonly used in the UK construction industry

3.18 The following cost definitions are commonly used in the UK construction industry and should be read as being in addition to the definitions provided in Section 8.

- **annual equivalent** the present value of a series of discounted cash flows expressed as a constant annual amount.
- **base cost, or benchmark cost** the existing or selected situation against which improvement options can be compared or a specific solution selected as a benchmark against which other options can be measured.
- **base rate** the interest rate selected as the basis of the discount rate. This could be the current bank rate or client's opportunity cost of capital. The base rate is commonly adjusted by the inflation rate to give the discount rate.
- **depreciation** the distribution of the monetary value of an asset over the period of time commonly related to its productive or useful life.

- **design life** intended service life, or expected service life, or service life intended by the designer.
- **discount rate** the interest rate used for bringing future costs to a comparable time base.
- **hard facilities management costs** the cost of necessary replacement, redecoration, repair and corrective, responsive and preventative maintenance necessary for the continued specified functional performance of the asset.
- **inflation/deflation** a sustained and measurable increase/decrease in the general price level.
- **internal rate of return** the discount rate that, when applied to a case flow containing positive and negative amounts, gives an NPV of zero.
- **physical life of a component** the time at which a component fails to meet the performance criteria required of it and has to be removed and replaced.
- **residual life** when applied to an asset it is that remaining at the end of the study period.
- **residual value** the value assigned to an asset at the end of the period of study.
- **service life** period of time after installation during which a building, or its part, meets or exceeds the performance requirements.
- **sinking fund** fund accumulated by equal payments made at regular time periods into an account which attracts a given interest rate to accumulate a required sum of money established prior to undertaking the sinking fund calculations.
- **soft facilities management costs** all costs incurred in operating and managing the facility or constructed assets, including administration support services, cleaning, security, rent, rates, insurances, energy, local taxes and charges etc.
- **sunk costs** costs of labour, goods and services already incurred or irrevocably committed.
- **terminal value** the scrap value of a component or asset at the point of its replacement.
- **Treasury discount rate** the rate specified as the discount rate by the Government Treasury to be used as the discount rate for public-sector whole life costing calculations.

3.19 There will be other cost definitions peculiar to a sector, or to the client's specific project funding and accounting protocols. For example, for the Building Schools for the Future programme, in order to comply with the project funding requirements, the construction costs are split into the base build costs, separate from other supplementary costs, such as:

- **abnormal costs**
  - work to the existing site (e.g. phasing, demolition, temporary accommodation, protection, tight site working arrangements etc.);
  - site investigation works (obstructions, site levels, contamination etc.);
  - foundations (extra over base build);
  - statutory bodies (e.g. planning, listed buildings, service connections, diversions);
  - environmental costs (e.g. acoustics standards, petrol interceptors, land drainage);

- **enhancement costs**
  - environmental treatment (e.g. solar panelling, triple glazing, new technologies);
  - security provisions (e.g. extra provisions for inner-city situations);
  - site landscaping (e.g. trim trail, running tracks etc.);
  - other user-definable items (e.g. additional teaching areas, extra car parking).

*Note: specific guidance on schools-sector cost structuring can be found on the Partnerships for Schools (PfS) website (www.p4s.org.uk).*

# APPLICATIONS 4

## Deciding the purpose and level of life cycle costing

4.1 Life cycle costing can be used for a variety of different purposes, for example:

- preliminary analysis to inform strategic investment decisions, or the budgetary process, e.g. to support a business case decision on whether or not to proceed with a project, to compare strategic options for the project or to set or test the budgets and affordability limits;
- to evaluate total building options, e.g. whether to choose a new build versus a refurbishment or compare alternative design and construction solutions for the project;
- to evaluate detailed design options at elemental, system, sub-elemental and component levels;
- to determine optimum maintenance and life cycle replacement (LCR) strategies;
- to analyze relocation strategies, e.g. whether to construct, lease or refurbish an existing asset;
- to determine and inform cyclical investment planning/sinking fund requirements, e.g. to finance and control the spend on future planned maintenance and capital replacement programmes;
- due diligence on the life cycle costing, e.g. for a project funder's assurance or for cost auditing.

*(Informative worked examples of two of these scenarios are included in Annex D.)*

4.2 Life cycle costing can be prepared at various stages of the project process, depending on the client's particular requirements and on the degree of detail and information available. The general principle that determines the level at which calculations of life cycle costing are made is the corresponding level of detail of the construction cost plan.

4.3 While the process of establishing the life cycle costing will be the same at each stage, the context in which it is being prepared will set the level of detail, the need for iterations, the need for component option appraisals, the type of report (i.e. specific outputs and format) and the requirement to share data and assumptions with others.

4.4 The different purposes for which life cycle costing may be deployed and the different stages of the asset life cycle at which it is used imply the need for different levels of detail and accuracy in the process.

4.5 The typical levels of life cycle costing used during the design development stages of a project are:

- **Setting the LCC budgets (Stage 1)** The first-generation LCC budgeting is normally undertaken at a whole-building level or by functional area or department during the initial project-investment concept and feasibility stages. It is expressed as cost per square metre of GIFA. Costs may be expressed as a percentage of construction cost, or annual equivalent pounds sterling per square metre, or as a cost per function (e.g. cost per bed space or cost per pupil).
- **Elemental life cycle costing (Stage 2)** This is commonly used for developing solutions at project level during option appraisals. Costs are normally at building elemental level on the entire asset. Information may be a mix of typical benchmark costs for key elements, comparative cost modelling or approximate estimates. It is expressed as cost

per square metre of GIFA and presented for elemental analysis, aligned to the level of capital cost plans.

- **Sub-elemental and component level life cycle costing (Stages 3 and 4)** These are commonly used for cost planning specification choices of systems, elements or component levels during design development. Costs to be included will depend on the purpose and scope of study agreed and the stage in the asset life cycle at which the study is carried out. (See Figure 4.1.)

4.6 Process map of the key stages when life cycle costing is typically undertaken over the construction life cycle.

*(See page 23.)*

## Typical applications of life cycle costing during a construction life cycle

4.7 Life cycle costing can be used at different stages of the project construction life cycle, for example:

- **During the investment planning stage**. Life cycle costing is used to provide a high-level economic prediction of the project's life cycle costs, to enable the client or property owner to make informed investment decisions regarding which project option is viable, sustainable and represents best value (this may be part of a wider whole life costing or sustainability and environment assessment). Life cycle costing can influence whether or not, finally, to commit to construction.
- **During conceptual planning and early stages of scheme design**. Life cycle costing is used as part of a strategic option appraisal process, to inform the selection of fundamental or to cost significant elements, such as structure, envelope, services etc.
- **During the detailed design stage**. To appraise and select the detailed design options from a life cycle cost and performance perspective and to optimize the LCC plan.
- **During the tendering**. To compare a bid's competitiveness and to test the project affordability.
- **During the construction and handover stages**. To set up the LCC in use budgets, based on life cycle cost planning using the construction and/or refurbishment costs.
- **During the lifetime use of the constructed asset**. To provide a detailed assessment of the life cycle costs in use during the operational period – e.g. refurbish versus asset renewal studies.
- **At hand-back stage**. At the end of life or period of interest, e.g. hand-back costs, residual value.

This publication provides instructions on the application of life cycle costing for Stages 1 to 4 only. Annex F provides a form for life cycle cost analysis purposes that will typically be used at Stages 5, 6 and 7.

*(At time of publication, a supplement for the post-project construction or 'asset' life cycle costing in use is planned, which will deal with the typical applications of life cycle costing for Stages 7, 8 and 9.)*

*Figure 4.1 Process map of the key stages when LCC is typically undertaken*

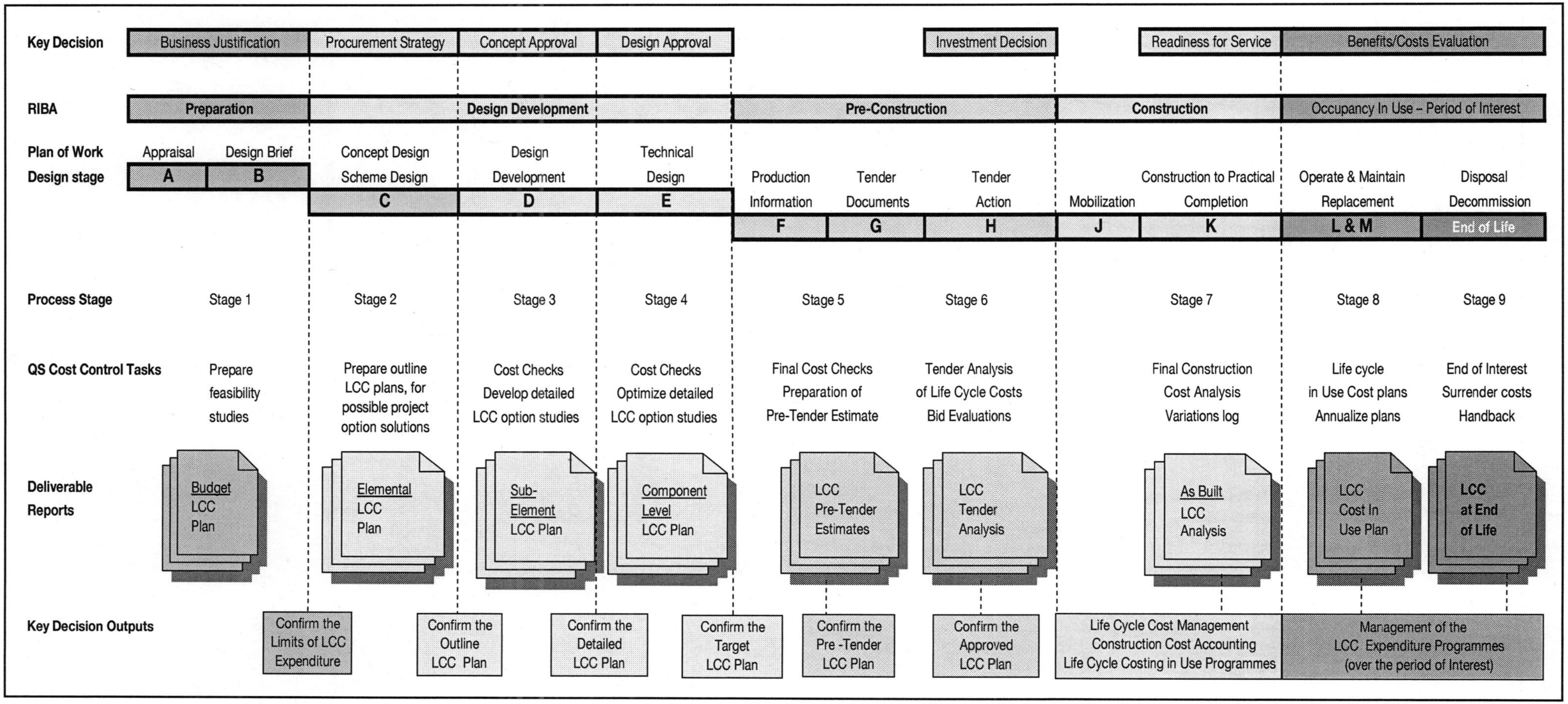

## Instructions for undertaking LCC planning and analysis

4.8 The purpose of the life cycle costing study should be agreed (i.e. the type of LCC study as in item 4.1, 4.7 and 4.45).

4.9 The client's specific form of output required from the LCC study shall be stated. Examples:

- prediction of a single LCC cash flow output: for comparing a number of possible options, which may be used to feed into a wider whole life costing or for budgeting exercise purposes;
- option appraisal, based on multiple cash flow scenarios: e.g. 25, 30, 60 or 100+ years;
- comparison of options, at various levels: for tenders or to identify the best-value option;
- audit of a single- or multiple-option appraisal: to check the adequacy and robustness;
- other outputs, as specifically defined by the client.

4.10 The precise scope of the life cycle costing shall be defined and agreed with the client, such as:

- stages over which the life cycle costing will be applied;
- the level of the study, which could be one or more of the levels of study, as defined in item 2.9;
- the period of analysis, including adjusting for the time value of money (e.g. NPV, payback period);
- the extent to which sustainability and wider WLC assessments relate to the life cycle costing;
- the project-specific design and life cycle performance requirements, including end-of-life cost;
- agree the project-specific options to be included in the life cycle costing study (e.g. types of cladding);
- establish what relevant information is available for the preparation of the life cycle costing;
- the need and extent of risks and uncertainty and the form of sensitivity analysis to be applied.

4.11 The scope of costing to be included or excluded from the life cycle costing assessment shall be stated, using the UK standard cost data structure for life cycle costing included in Section 3.

4.12 Cost for infrastructure and external works shall be shown separately.

4.13 If there is more than one building or functional facility in a constructed asset, the individual cost plans can be aggregated for reporting purposes.

4.14 Items not included in the construction cost plan that shall be included in the life cycle costing should be shown separately, e.g. client- or occupant-supplied furniture, fittings and equipment.

4.15 Other construction items, not part of the project capital cost plan, which will have to be maintained or replaced, will need to be included in the study, e.g. the existing roads, if included in scope.

4.16 The precise period of the life cycle costing study shall be stated. The period is the time from the agreed base date year to a given point in time in the future, and over which the calculations pertain.

4.17 Base date year shall be stated, i.e. the point in time from which the life cycle costing period commences. All relevant costs used for the life cycle costing study shall be adjusted to the base date for comparative prediction purposes, e.g. construction, operation, maintenance and replacement etc.

4.18 The unit of time shall be stated. The units of time are the increments to which the calculations refer, e.g. years, six-monthly intervals, months, weeks or days. All factors in the calculations, e.g. interest rates, will relate to the stated unit of time.

4.19 Assumptions relating to interest rates and discount rates shall be stated if required.

4.20 The method of depreciation shall be stated. Where depreciation is not applicable, this shall be stated.

4.21 The LCC study must state whether the data used have been built up from first principles or whether comparative and benchmark data have been used, stating the source (client historic data, manufacturer literature etc.).

4.22 When specific information sources are used, then the source and any assumptions should be stated, for example:

- client requirements and performance data (e.g. BRE Environmental Assessment Method (BREEAM) rating: excellent);
- industry standards for planned preventative maintenance schedules (e.g. Heating and Ventilation Contractors' Association (HVCA) Service Facilities Group (SFG) 2008 revision);
- published information on expected life cycle replacement (RICS, CIBSE etc.);
- consultants' internal data or particular experience.

4.23 Information should be input into the LCC plan in a structured way so that, as far as possible, the same approach is adopted for all the LCC cash flow and option appraisals. This will assist with the aim of allowing meaningful comparison and data sharing.

4.24 Assumptions with regard to end-of-interest or end-of-life activities in the final period of the assessment shall be stated.

4.25 Assumptions with regard to residual values in the final year shall be stated, e.g. a straight-line method of depreciation may be assumed.

4.26 The method or techniques and the criteria used for undertaking sensitivity analysis and/or risk analysis shall be stated, e.g. discount rates, factoring component service lives, cost-significant items modelling.

4.27 Sources of design and service life data for component replacement should be stated, together with confirmation of the predicted range of replacement life used and the associated basis for factoring these to relate them to the specific project circumstances, e.g. failure or obsolescence, which may be:

- physical;
- economic;
- functional;
- technological;
- social;
- legal.

*(See Section 6.17 for more guidance on service life-expectancy planning and factoring methods.)*

## Presentation of the costs and the methods of economic evaluation

4.28 The presentation of costs will depend on the client's specific requirements. There are two typical methods of presenting the costs commonly used in the UK construction industry:

1. A discounted cash flow is normally required for public-sector clients (in accordance with public-sector investment appraisal guidance, discount rates etc.) or for occasional clients (where the analysis should include justification of the selected discount rate, period of analysis etc.).

2. A cash flow (at the base date prices), which is not discounted. This is typically used where the LCC analysis feeds into separate economic assessment, i.e. the discounting is dealt with as part of the wider whole life costing economic evaluation.

If discounting is required, costs should be calculated by taking costs that occur in future years and reducing them by a discount factor derived from the discount rate.

4.29 Present value (for option appraisal) is defined as the amount to be invested in the bank today to pay for all future costs at a given interest rate over a known time horizon. A stream of future costs can be converted to a Present Value (PV) by summing the results of:

$$PV = \frac{\text{Future Cost in year } N}{(1 + \text{Discount percentage}) \times N}$$

($N$ = number of years between the base date and occurrence of the cost.)

The net present value (NPV) should be a single figure that takes account of all relevant future incomes and expenditure over the period of analysis. NPV is the normal measure used in a discounted LCC analysis, although others are available.

4.30 BS ISO 15686-5 defines other methods of economic evaluation, such as payback period (PB), net savings (NS), savings to investment ratio (SIR), internal rate of return (IRR) and annual equivalent cost (AEC). BS ISO 15686-5, Annex B, provides examples of calculating costs for the various methods of economic evaluation.

4.31 Life cycle costing calculation intervals should be stated, i.e. six-monthly, annually, periodically or in cyclical years.

4.32 Where costs are required to be presented in an adjusted form (NPV etc.), they should also be reported in current cash terms and should state if they are smoothed or unsmoothed cash-flow profiles.

## Discount rate and escalation rates

4.33 The discount rate is a key variable in life cycle costing. Real discount rates are used with future costs which are estimated at present values. This involves an assumption that inflation/deflation applies equally to all. Nominal rates involve an estimate of what future costs will be (and they typically therefore include an element for inflation). Escalation rates may also be used, where there are grounds to anticipate that the standard rate of inflation will not apply in the case of a specific option. Typically, real rates should be used as they build on the estimator's understanding of current conditions and cost inputs. Nominal rates may be used by agreement, if that is what the client requires or if the situation justifies it.

4.34 Within the UK public sector, a discount rate might be determined by central government (sometimes termed 'social discount rates') as a test requirement for their investments, based on an assessment of the long-term opportunity cost to the public sector of selecting one investment rather than another.

4.35 The discount rate in the private sector should represent the opportunity cost of investing the capital, which might be:

- the interest cost of a loan for the investment;
- the interest lost on reduction of cash on deposit;
- returns lost on investment elsewhere (e.g. in bonds or equities);
- the risk and uncertainty of the proposed investment;
- the actual return achieved on capital investment in the business;
- the required investor's rate of return in a business involving the constructed asset.

4.36 Where the discount rate is not a fixed requirement by the client (public or private), it is normal to undertake sensitivity analysis on a range of rates to test the validity of the conclusions if input conditions change.

## Interpretation and presenting the results

4.37 The results of an LCC plan should be documented in a report so that they are clearly presented in accordance with the pre-agreed scoping and the client's required outputs and reporting requirements. BS ISO 15686-5: Section 9 provides guidance on what the report should include and how to present it.

4.38 The key things to consider when interpreting and presenting the initial results of the life cycle costing are:

- Verify and confirm the financial parameters and period of analysis used and any taxation issues etc.
- Check and validate the cost calculations and discount formula etc. used to generate the life cycle costing.
- Spot check all the most cost-significant elements and key information and data assumptions used, such as service life expectancy or replacement cycles, and run further iterations as required.
- Carry out detailed risk and uncertainty analysis (as required). Refer to Section 6 for more guidance.
- Carry out additional sensitivity analysis (as required). Refer to Sections 5 and 6 for more guidance.
- Present the initial results using cash-flow programmes, tables and graphical representations to aid the understanding and to provide a readily comprehensible summary of the results.

- Obtain formal client approval of the final results and then prepare and issue a controlled copy of the final report, which clearly records the basis upon which the LCC plan was produced.

*(Examples of how to present the results are shown in the worked examples included in Annex D.)*

## How the LCC methodology supports wider sustainability assessments

4.39 Sustainability is now a critical consideration affecting the design, construction, operation and maintenance through to the disposal of the building or constructed asset. The life cycle costing methodology is a key element in assessing the sustainability of the built environment and is also an integral part of the wider business case, from a whole-life costing and best-value perspective.

4.40 The environmental impact of constructing, operating and maintaining the built environment is a particularly important element of sustainability. In general, the materials and products used in construction cause environmental impacts throughout the asset's life cycle process from manufacture, transport, assembly or disassembly, maintenance and decommissioning and or disposal. Additionally, constructed facilities generate a significant environmental impact in their own right due to the operations carried out during their in-use phase. Taken together, these environmental impacts are highly significant and should be addressed at the design and project planning stage of the construction project procurement.

4.41 The life cycle costing methodology set out in this document allows for the assessment of the economic cost effects of sustainability, notably energy and environmental considerations (i.e. key aspects of the option appraisals) so that the output provides a balanced basis for making informed decisions based on a sustainable economic evaluation, not just lowest initial capital costs. A key part of the life cycle costing study should be to identify, understand and then seek to mitigate or reduce the environmental impact whilst also taking account of relevant social economic considerations and thereby to support better the decision-making process from a sustainable construction perspective.

4.42 It is important to note that life cycle costing is an economic evaluation technique and its primary driver in informing the decision maker is cost. Other techniques are used, such as life cycle assessment (LCA). As defined by BS EN ISO 14040, LCA provides 'a systematic set of procedures for compiling and examining the inputs and outputs of materials and energy and the associated environmental impacts directly attributable to the functioning of a product or service system throughout its life cycle.' (adapted from BS EN ISO 14040, 3.2)

4.43 Life cycle costing, therefore, forms only a part of a wider whole life costing and sustainable construction assessment. It is important, however, to ensure that real cost implications of environmental and social impacts are fully understood and appropriately accounted for in the LCC planning. This will help to ensure that the best-value solutions in both economic and sustainability terms are identified.

4.44 Particular consideration should be given to assessing the key social and environmental aspects against specific targets (i.e. set by legislation or by the client in the project brief), notable energy performance of buildings and the carbon dioxide emissions.

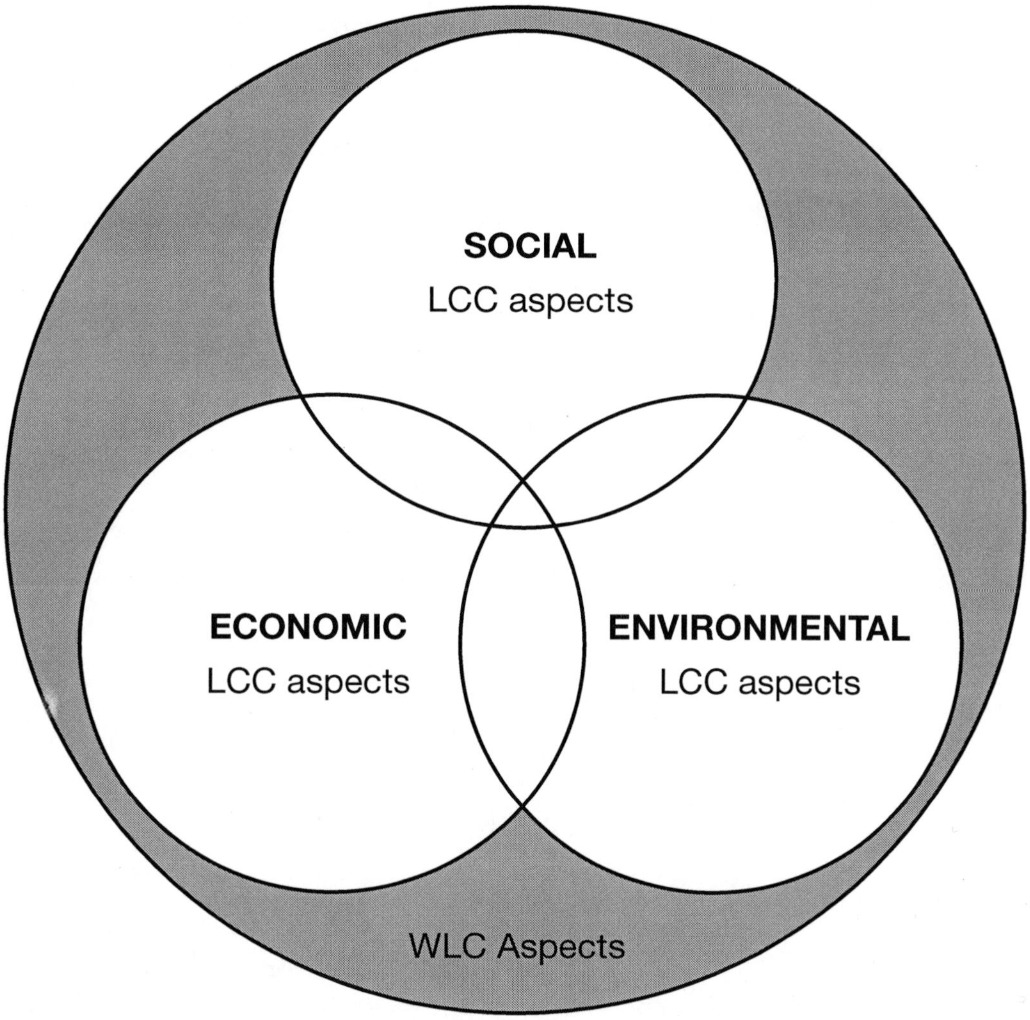


*Figure 4.2 Relationship of life cycle costs to WLCs, social and environment economic aspects.*

## Instructions on how to define the client's specific LCC study requirements

4.45 Table 4.1 provides a checklist for how to define the client requirements for undertaking a LCC plan.

*Table 4.1 Instructions on how to define specific LCC study requirements*

| | Key Activities | Instructions/Planned Outcomes |
|---|---|---|
| 1 | Define and agree the prime purpose and the output requirements for the life cycle costing (e.g. cash-flow, option appraisal, audit or budget setting or others as defined by the client). | Statement of the client's particular requirements. Understanding of the key objectives of the life cycle costing, i.e. application and form of the related outcomes required. |
| 2 | Identify the precise scope of the life cycle costing. | Determine: scale of LCC application: stages over which it will be applied; level of detail; period of the analysis; methods of economic evaluation (NPV); risk analysis etc. |
| 3 | Identify the extent to which the sustainability and any other wider analysis (e.g. whole life costing) relates to the life cycle costing. | Understanding of the relationship between the LCC and other sustainability assessments – in terms of defining the extent to which any wider WLC and/or sustainability assessment will form an input into the LCC process and vice versa – in economic terms (e.g. reducing energy consumption costs by introducing new technologies). |
| 4 | Identify the project particular design and life cycle performance requirements – including end of life considerations. | Definition of the construction project and key features – including construction project details (as SFCA), list of the project constraints and risks and opportunities; definition of relevant service life performance, quality and functional requirements etc; confirmation of the client's project budget and timetable. |
| 5 | Decide the project specific options to be included in the life cycle costing exercise and select the cost items to be considered. | Identify the boundary of the option study and also the key assets or elements to focus on in the LCC analysis (e.g. comparing alternative cladding product types) |
| 6 | Establish what relevant information is available for the preparation of the life cycle costing. | Compile and document all the available information and data sources to be used for the life cycle costing. |
| 7 | Establish the level of life cycle costing that is relevant to the stage of the project and to the information and time available (e.g. functional unit cost/beds, or elemental or detailed LCC planning). | The level of life cycle costing at each stage should be an amplification of the costs in the preceding stage. At any stage it should include any key cost significant items that are important for proper and robust analysis. |
| 8 | Identify the need and extent of additional analyses (i.e. uncertainty and risks and other factoring methods and sensitivity analysis). | Produce a life cycle costing risk log – then decide the appropriate use of 'factoring' methods and mitigation risk modelling and sensitivity analysis – to model the impact of the risks/variability items against the LCC base model prediction. |
| 9 | Assemble the units of cost, quality and time data (e.g. functional cost – GIFA or cost GIFA per annum). | Compile all the cost information relevant to do an LCC plan, including values for each cost item, any on-costs to be applied. Time related data (e.g. service life expectancy and maintenance programme data etc). |
| 10 | Record all assumptions, methods, data sources and definitions of terms to be used for life cycle costing – and document in the project LCC report. | Document all assumptions and related cost definitions and customize them to suit the specific project details. |

# METRICS 5

## Types of 'Metrics' used for life cycle costing of a building or constructed asset

5.1 The economic evaluation of life cycle costing in practice will be measured and reported using a variety of metrics, depending on the actual purpose, project stage and relevant use, level of detail and type of study being undertaken.

5.2 The key metrics used for life cycle costing in construction procurement are listed in Table 5.1.

*Table 5.1 Types of metrics used for life cycle costing of a building or constructed asset*

| **TOTAL LIFE CYCLE COSTS (LCC)** | Total LCC £ – at base date prices, or net present value (NPV) or other form of economic evaluation. |
|---|---|
| Other methods of economic evaluation | Net savings (NS); payback period (PB), internal rate of return (IRR) annual equivalent cost (AEC). |
| Derived indicators | LCC £ per $m^2$ (GIFA) and LCC per functional unit (e.g. cost per bed space, pupil, workspace etc.). |
| **RATIOS** | LCC as % of construction cost – also the life cycle replacement costs as % of the construction costs. |
| **ANNUAL EQUIVALENT LCC** | Total LCC in pounds sterling £ per annum.<br>Elemental total LCC pounds sterling £ per annum. |
| Derived indicators | Total LCC £ per $m^2$ (GIFA) per annum<br>Elemental total LCC £ per $m^2$ per annum |
| Typical life cycle costing analysis | Calculated on net building costs and also on gross construction costs, including all on-costs in scope.<br>Splits in capital costs, life cycle replacement costs, and by operation, maintenance and occupancy and end of life costs, plus other costs (in scope). |
| **Supplementary supporting information** | |
| BCIS detailed facility or building classification listing (e.g. secondary school, not just school). | |
| Base dates for the construction start and end and also dates for all the life cycle replacement, operation maintenance occupancy costing periods. | |
| Indexation indices applied in generating the total LCC (e.g. to uplift the life cycle cost estimates for the location factors and tender price adjustment). | |
| The period of analysis (e.g. 25 years). Note: including any liabilities beyond this period that have been reflected in the costing – e.g. hand-back liabilities stated in the contractual agreement. | |
| Whether the scope of life cycle costing is standard or includes/excludes project specific areas (e.g. furniture, incomes, business occupancy costs etc.). | |
| Reported in current real cash terms (or in Net Present Value terms. If it is discounted, then state the discount rate used). | |
| Whether the figures reported include or exclude any sensitivity analysis and risk allowances. | |

## Key indicator definitions

5.3 Total LCC is the prime metric and measure and should be provided as well as any of the other indicators. Reporting of the total LCCs should include the relevant supporting information.

5.4 LCC per square metre is derived from the total LCC but is expressed per metre of GIFA.

5.5 LCC per functional unit is a report of the total LCC expressed on the basis of the primary form of accommodation provided, e.g. bed spaces (housing and healthcare), cells or inmates (prisons), pupils (education), desk spaces (commercial offices) etc.

## Ratios

5.6 LCC as a percentage of construction cost: this ratio gives an indication of the balance between the capital construction costs and the operation, maintenance, occupancy and end of life costs etc. (in scope).

5.7 Construction cost as a percentage of total LCC: this is similar to the ratio above but is highly relevant where initial costs are capped or when preparing a life cycle costing for a refurbishment of an existing built asset.

5.8 Life cycle replacement costs as a percentage of total construction cost: this is similar to the ratio above but for life cycle replacement costs only, excluding preventative and unscheduled maintenance, operation, occupancy costs and end of life costs.

## Annual equivalent LCCs

5.9 Annual LCC: this is derived from total LCC divided by the time period of analysis, i.e. number of years.

5.10 Annual LCC per annum per square metre: this is also derived from total LCC and the period of analysis and is expressed per metre of GIFA.

5.11 Annual LCC per functional unit: this is derived from total LCC and the period of analysis and is expressed per unit of the primary form of accommodation.

## Typical cost breakdown analysis

5.12 Capital construction costs (Capex)

**Total:** this is the elemental total cost of the Capex works (which could be new build and or a refurbishment).
**Total per square metre:** this is the total Capex divided by the GIFA and expressed in square metres ($m^2$).
**New build:** this is the total costs for the new element of the building or constructed asset.
**New build per square metre:** this is the new build cost divided by the GIFA (in square metres).
**Percentage new:** this is the Capex total cost including new and refurbishment, divided by Capex total new cost.

5.13 LCR costs

**Total:** this is the total estimated LCR cost for the whole period of study (excluding annualized planned preventative maintenance (PPM), reliability centred maintenance and provision for unscheduled reactive maintenance, and all the operations and occupancy costs).

**Percentage new:** this is the total LCR cost by the new build, expressed as a percentage of Capex, as the Capex could be minimal on a refurbishment and therefore misleading.
**Elemental £/m²:** this is an elemental costing of the LCR costs divided by the GIFA.
**NPV:** this is the net present value of the total LCR cost.
**NPV/m²:** this is the NPV divided by the GIFA expressed in square metres.

5.14 Total LCCs

**Total:** this is the total estimated LCC for the whole period of study. It excludes any costs not required beyond the end of the period of study but includes any costs to meet hand-back obligations or residual life requirements.
**Percentage new:** this is the total LCC divided by the new build cost, expressed as a percentage (not a percentage of Capex as the Capex could be minimal on a refurbishment).
**NPV:** this is the net present value of the total LCR cost.
**NPV/m²:** this is the NPV divided by the GIFA expressed in square metres.

# RISKS AND UNCERTAINTY 6

## Why do risks and uncertainty need to be considered?

6.1 Life cycle costing deals with future costs. Therefore, there are degrees of variability, i.e. risks and uncertainty, regarding the work items, quantities, rates, information and the service lives used, which affect the accuracy and robustness of the predictions. The life cycle costing should clearly state what is included and excluded from the analysis, but client decision-makers may still need assistance to understand the critical nature of key information and assumptions and the sensitivity of the results to changing decision variables (e.g. large rises in energy-consumption levels, early asset failure, significant rises in excess of forecasted labour rates and energy prices).

6.2 This section seeks to illustrate the key areas of risk and uncertainty, along with potential consequences that impact on the decision-making. A brief overview is provided in this section of a number of industry-accepted techniques, i.e. risk management and sensitivity techniques, together with guidance on how they can be used to help minimize the risks and uncertainties and improve the confidence in the outputs from the life cycle costing study. These techniques apply equally to the capital cost planning.

## What risks and uncertainties need to be considered?

6.3 There are a number of key uncertainties and risks that should be taken into account when undertaking any life cycle costing study. These uncertainties and risks can arise as a result of variability in one or more of the predicted values or assumptions used in generating the life cycle costing analysis. Typical examples of variability are:

- capital costs (actual versus predicted);
- operational costs including maintenance cycles (annual expenditure provision versus actual life cycle maintenance and replacement plans);
- operational usage (actual usage changes versus forecast planned usage defined in the LCC plan);
- the level of complexity of the design;
- design quality and workmanship quality;
- costs of refurbishment/upgrade;
- quality of refurbishment/upgrade;
- energy-consumption levels;
- energy market price rises;
- economic obsolescence;
- technology obsolescence;
- social obsolescence;
- environmental targets required to comply with sustainability drivers;
- future levels of labour wage rises (impacting on labour and material costs);
- service live predictions not achieved in practice;
- availability and robustness of historical benchmarking on cost and performance data;
- variations: changes to the project stakeholder's particular requirements/period of interest.

## Identification of the causes of risks and uncertainty

6.4 The identification and assessment of risks and uncertainty can have a significant influence on the decision-making, as a result of the impact of variables on the life cycle costing study.

6.5 The level of uncertainty and risk associated with life cycle costing can depend on such issues as the quality of the data available, the robustness of the scoping and pricing of LCCs, the service life expectancy assumptions and the methods of calculations and sensitivity analysis used.

6.6 In order to address cost uncertainty and to mitigate risks, the key issues and barriers to life cycle costing being widely used should be understood. Issues that should be considered in LCC analysis are broadly defined in BS ISO 15685-5, 8.2.

## Life cycle costing risks log

6.7 Annex E in this publication includes an example of a life cycle costing risk log, which provides a listing of the typical risks that are commonly encountered when undertaking a life cycle costing study.

## Risk and sensitivity analysis techniques used to mitigate the risks and uncertainty

6.8 All the relevant techniques commonly used for mitigating risk and uncertainty in construction cost planning should also be applied to LCC planning, e.g. risk and value management.

6.9 BS ISO 15658-5 defines various statistical techniques used to mitigate the risks and uncertainty:

- Monte Carlo analysis and confidence modelling (refer to BS ISO 15686-5, 8.3);
- sensitivity analysis for modelling the effects of changing key assumptions (refer to BS ISO 15686-5, 8.4).

6.10 Specific consideration should be given to testing the impact on the LCC plan of various inputs such as:

- service life expectancy and replacement cycles;
- costing of the replacement cycles;
- discount rates (if applicable).

6.11 The impact of changing individual variables is tested by changing a single variable at a time, often within a range of possible values (i.e. worse case, best case and most likely case) to improve confidence levels. This allows the criticality of particular cost-significant items or assumptions to be tested.

## Service life expectancy: replacement cycles and the factoring method

6.12 RICS Life Expectancy Schedules and the CIBSE Equipment Service Life Data (in Section 13 of Guide M) and other reference sources listed in the bibliography in Annex G, provide the industry-recognized sources for expected reference service lives (RSL) for life cycle costing of major repairs and replacement programmes. These are indicative lives and should be used with caution, and they assume that appropriate maintenance will be undertaken. In any event, consideration should be given to the operational environment in which the asset is used. A hospital, for example, is in full operation for twenty-four hours every day, and, therefore, would have higher usage of a particular asset than, say, a school.

6.13 Default or RSL for components and materials represents a particular set of assumptions that should be recorded in the data source. These assumptions are unlikely to replicate exactly the project conditions, and, therefore, the service lives will need to be adjusted to represent the likely actual life in service conditions. Some RSLs are also quoted as at least *X* years or are limited to a minimum estimate (e.g. sixty years) so may need to be adjusted or varied by suitably experienced life cycle practitioners.

## Replacement cycles and how to apply the factoring method

6.14 Part 1 and Part 8 of BS ISO 15686 deal with how to factor estimates of component service lives. The default assumption is that the value of each factor is 1.

6.15 Where the project conditions are worse than assumed in the reference case, use a value of less than 1 (typically 0.9 or 0.8) for each relevant factor.

6.16 Where the project conditions are better than assumed in the reference case, use a value of more than 1 (typically 1.1 or 1.2) for each relevant factor.

6.17 Consider whether the conditions are cumulatively adequately represented by the revised estimate of service lives. Note that different components and materials will be more or less sensitive to particular factors, such as in-use asset conditions.

*Table 6.1 Example of factoring the reference service life (RSL).*

| Factors | RSL Assumption | Project Conditions |
|---|---|---|
| A: quality of components | Reference service life for windows | High quality specification, assume 1.1 |
| B: design level | Not stated | Assume 1 |
| C: work execution level | In accordance with good practice | Assume 1 |
| D: indoor environment | Not applicable | Not applicable |
| E: outdoor environment | South-East of England | East coast of Scotland, exposed to more aggressive climate, assume 0.8 |
| F: in-use conditions | External envelope | External envelope, assume 1 |
| G: maintenance level | Regular cleaning | None, assume 0.8 |
| Resultant values | 1 | **1.1 x 0.8 x 0.8 = 0.704** |

## Example of factoring the RSL

6.18 In this case, the RSL should be reduced by multiplying it by 0.704 (or reduced by 30 per cent), recognizing that the value of factoring lies not in the absolute values calculated but in the process of evaluating the factors applicable.

*More examples are provided in BS ISO 15686-1, and more detailed evaluation techniques will be provided in BS ISO 15686-8.*

## Monitoring the detailed design and construction phases

6.19 In Figure 4.1 of this publication, the process of life cycle costing is shown in the context of Stages A–K of the RIBA plan of work. Fundamentally, it is a generally iterative process, and the accuracy of prediction improves as the design develops from feasibility through to production information and finally the actual installation.

6.20 Many assumptions are made including, not least, costs and component service lives. By the start of the construction phase, capital costs, as distinct from future costs, become reasonably certain (future change orders not withstanding). In contrast, component lives may be considered less certain. In Sections 6.12 to 6.18, the use of Factors A–G to fine-tune service life predictions is explained. Factors A, B and C offer the potential for improving certainty during the construction phase.

6.21 Factor A (quality of components): a factor may have been applied to the RSL to reflect that a high-quality component was envisaged (or equally a basic quality). The process of translating such an assumption into a deliverable has associated practical risks, including:

- original performance specification not reflected in what the constructor actually orders;
- named components found to have unacceptable lead times and the constructor makes a substitution of an alternative with unconfirmed performance;
- specification too open-ended, allowing lesser quality components to be utilized;
- constructors being given freedom to select 'equal or approved', but, through lack of knowledge or expertise, select something that is less than equal.

6.22 From the moment that a component arrives on site, it becomes possible to substitute a 'factored' service life for an 'absolute' service life, where suitable protocols are in place to monitor materials at the point of fixing. Associated assumptions should also be confirmed such as quality of fixings (e.g. plated steel nails rather than copper nails).

6.23 Factor B (design level): a factor may have been applied to an RSL to reflect the anticipated attention to the design detail. Even if a default value of 1 has been applied, the RSL will be based on an assumption that good design practice would be followed. Experience indicates that this is an optimistic assumption in some situations as a consequence of, for example:

- the scope of the designer's brief being limited to 'outline design' only and reliance placed on site skills to work out the detail;
- the designers not being fully aware of the criticality of certain design issues associated with less common materials or components;
- an inadequate coordination of design as undertaken by various independent specialists;
- the use of untried innovative design and technology;
- a reliance placed on third parties such as building control or latent defects insurers to check out the design.

6.24 Use of designers and other specialists with certified Quality Assurance (QA) procedures and clear evidence of relevant life cycle costing and risk experience can give some comfort to clients. Independent expert verification and checking may be contemplated where the risks of premature failure are significant. Clients minimizing professional design and other specialist fees during Stages 1 to 4 should be regarded as increasing risks of premature component failure and increased LCCs.

6.25 Factor C (work execution level): a negative or positive factor may be applied to an RSL to reflect the anticipated quality of workmanship. Traditionally, construction clients have managed this risk by employing 'clerks of work' (or similar) to monitor site quality and so ensure compliance with contract specifications. The potential for less than adequate workmanship is well recognized:

- lack of skill, care or knowledge within site supervision and site operatives, heightened by the current skills shortage in the UK construction sector;
- reduced budgets for clerk of works-type inspection services;
- sub-contract type procurement of labour with reduced long-term accountability;

6.26 In the absence of suitable safeguards to ensure quality of installation (e.g. employment of a full-time clerk of works), then application of a negative work execution factor would be appropriate.

*Reference should be made to BS ISO 15686-3: 2002 for guidance on the operation of formal technical auditing processes in respect of Factors A, B and C.*

# INFORMATION AND DATA ASSUMPTIONS 7

## Information and data assumptions used for undertaking life cycle costing

7.1 The level of project information data needed to produce an LCC study will vary depending on the purpose, use of the LCC output, scope of costs and the stage in the project.

7.2 The *Standardized Method for Life Cycle Costing* (SMLCC) provides guidance on the relevant project information to be recorded. The following headings should normally be dealt with as indicated in Table 7.1. Exceptions to the items noted in this table should be stated in the report where they affect the life cycle costing. Note that not all of this information will be required for every type of LCC study.

7.3 Specific project information and data sources should be obtained from the client, the project teams and/or industry sources and made totally transparent during the generation and reporting of the LCC plan.

*Table 7.1 Information and data assumptions used for undertaking life cycle costing*

| LCC Descriptor | Project Information and Data Sources – (as applicable) |
|---|---|
| Project details and the named parties involved | State project details and the names and contact details of all key parties involved in providing information relevant to the life cycle costing study. |
| Purpose and required reporting outputs from the life cycle cost study | State the specific use of the life cycle costing study and required outputs:<br>• Whether the LCC plan is to be used for a business case study, for option appraisal (i.e. for public sector shall be in accordance with Office of Government Commerce OGC gateway process), or for producing a cash-flow for a sinking fund or other stated purpose<br>• Any specific requirements in respect of reporting (e.g. basis of economic evaluation – net present value, payback period etc.) |
| Level of risk analysis (if required) | • Any specific level of risk to be assessed (e.g. maximum/minimum/most likely, and/or 10:50:80% confidence levels). |
| Scope of the costs | State what costs are to be included or excluded and how to express them. |
| Base date(s) | State the base dates for the life cycle costing and the basis for indexation:<br>• Base date for pricing the life cycle costing study<br>• Construction start/completion dates<br>• Life cycle replacement start and end dates (period of study)<br>• Maintenance start and end dates (period of study)<br>• Operation start and end dates (period of study)<br>• Occupancy start and end dates (period of study)<br>• End of life (date and any period of liability beyond)<br>• Location factors and tender price adjustment (using BCIS indices). |

| LCC Descriptor | Project Information and Data Sources – (as applicable) |
|---|---|
| Time (period of analysis) | State:<br>• Period of analysis<br>• Any hand-back liability period beyond the period of study (e.g. boilers to have a minimum 5 further years service life expectancy)<br>• Construction and handover dates<br>• Phasing/sections if applicable<br>• Total asset life expectancy<br>• Basis of years (i.e. calendar, financial etc.)<br><br>How construction costs have been treated (e.g. all in year zero, pro-rata over a period etc.). |
| Procurement route and market conditions | State:<br>• Contractual procurement route ( e.g. Design and Build and Operate Maintain – with or without finance etc., as in PFI and other forms)<br>• Procurement stage (e.g. initial feasibility, outline design, per-tender)<br>• Market conditions<br>• Tender basis. |
| Project specific options (for option appraisals) | State specific options to be considered in the life cycle costing study (e.g. types of cladding systems compared with a traditional brick and block cavity option). |
| Location | State where the project is. |
| Level of design (stage) | State the level of design on which the LCC is to be based (e.g. conceptual). |
| Environment targets (for economic evaluation) | Any requirements for the building, e.g. notably the specific building energy performance targets; BREEAM rating (excellent); $CO_2$ emission targets – and any other social or environmental economic aspects to be considered. |
| Details of the building accommodation and design features<br><br>*(as normally provided for a capital cost analysis)* | Brief description of the building and include (when available) floor plans, sections, specifications, structural drawings, services etc. (as BCIS SFCA)<br>• Outline specifications<br>• Floor areas (GIFA)<br>• Number of storeys<br>• Storey heights<br>• Basement floors<br>• Wall to floor ratio<br>• Element ratios<br>• Functional units<br>• Internal cube<br>• External wall area<br>• Usable area<br>• Circulation area |

| LCC Descriptor | Project Information and Data Sources – (as applicable) |
|---|---|
| Details of the building accommodation and design features (continued) | • Ancillary areas<br>• Internal divisions<br>• Areas of glazing<br>• Other areas requiring regular cleaning<br>• Site area overall (m$^2$) and the area of hard landscaping (m$^2$). |
| Intended occupancy use | State:<br><br>• Assumptions about the intended use of the building or facility<br>• Hours of operation/intended use<br>• Peak operation points/length of peaks. |
| Documentation used for the actual LCC study | State:<br><br>• List of documents forming the basis of the LCC study (both the project documents and external documents – e.g. product literature)<br>• Sources of data used (e.g. project specific + in the public domain) |
| Sunk costs (excluded) | Sunk costs – are the costs of goods and services already incurred or irrevocably committed. They should be excluded from the LCC plan. |
| Capital expenditure context | The context of the capital cost plan and how it will be used to generate the life cycle costing. |
| Construction costs | The instructions in the BCIS Standard Form of Cost Analysis (SFCA) should be followed. Construction related costs not covered by the SFCA, such as consultancy fees, contingencies etc., shall be included (see '1.2 Construction related costs' in Table 3.1) – including the cost of initial investment in occupancy related items such as furniture, fittings and equipment (FF&E) and information and communication technology (ICT). |
| Major replacements | State:<br><br>• Client requirements (e.g. meeting all legal obligations, Corporate Social Responsibility and business critical maintenance tailored to, functional failure impacts, image/reputation considerations etc.)<br>• Standards required to be maintained (e.g. condition/performance)<br>• Working restrictions (e.g. access hours etc.)<br>• Allowance for associated work to undertake the replacement<br>• Procurement context (e.g. direct labour, outsourced).<br><br>*Note: The cost of replacement and maintenance will be influenced by the hours of operation of the building.*<br><br>Document and agree with the interested parties the interface between the major replacement costs, minor replacement and repair costs; and the unscheduled replacement, repairs and maintenance costs (e.g. contractual boundary agreement between 'hard FM' and the 'life cycle renewal funds'). |

| LCC Descriptor | Project Information and Data Sources – (as applicable) |
|---|---|
| Minor replacement, repairs and maintenance costs | State:<br><br>• Client requirements<br>• Standards required<br>• Working restrictions<br>• Procurement context (e.g. direct labour, outsourced)<br>• Provision for unscheduled maintenance<br>• Insurance considerations<br>• Others – user definable. |
| Subsequent refurbishment and adaptation costs (Note – if required to include in the period of LCC analysis) | State:<br><br>• Client requirements<br>• Standards required to be satisfied (condition/performance regime)<br>• Allowance for associated costs to undertake the refurbishment<br>• Procurement context (e.g. direct labour, outsourced). |
| End of life costs | State<br><br>• Client requirements<br>• Allowance for dilapidations; reinstatement to meet contractual requirements<br>• Allowance for outstanding maintenance, reduced life etc.<br>• Disposal inspections<br>• Any special disposal costs (e.g. nuclear waste, batteries etc.)<br>• Requirement for demolition of the building if this is covered by the period of analysis. |
| Operation – Cleaning | State:<br><br>• Client requirements<br>• Standards required<br>• Working restrictions<br>• Procurement context (e.g. direct labour, outsourced)<br>• Physical environment for external cleaning (e.g. availability of cradle systems etc.). |
| Operation – Utilities | State:<br><br>• Pricing context<br>• Units (e.g. KW/hour/p.a.)<br>• Allowances for standing charges. |
| Administrative costs *(for maintenance operations and occupancy elements, as applicable)* | The following issues are to be included for LCC plans (where applicable):<br><br>• Supervisory and technical support staff (in house and consultancy)<br>• Security staff related to the building – (note the security system costs are to be included in maintenance costs)<br>• Services attendance, porters, site managers – (i.e. persons who are responsible for day to day maintenance – e.g. caretakers)<br>• Laundry (include only items normally supplied as part of the building contract, e.g. roller towels) |

| LCC Descriptor | Project Information and Data Sources – (as applicable) |
|---|---|
| Administrative costs (continued) | • Waste disposal (general waste, recycling, special waste)<br>• Property management (facilities management, FM stores, general management, administration cost, regulatory, general inspections). |
| Property insurance | Property insurance should be included.<br>Other insurance payable as part of the normal carrying out of work should be included with the work to which they relate. |
| Tax ( if applicable) | *Note the following (if taxes are included in the life cycle cost plan):*<br><br>• Rates should be included.<br>• VAT should be excluded (or if included must be stated separately).<br>• Taxes payable as part of the normal carrying out of work should be included with the work to which they relate.<br>• Effect on client's tax would normally form part of separate advice.<br>• Any allowances for the impact on client's tax included in the life cycle costing should be stated separately. |
| Occupancy costs | State:<br><br>• Any items included (see Section 3.4 occupancy cost elements)<br>• Client requirements<br>• Source of costs<br>(refer to Section 3.5 'occupancy costs to be included in the LCC study). |
| Future legislation | The LCC plan should only include allowances for legislation that has been enacted and this should be stated. Assumptions about future legislation that has not been enacted that are required to be included should be shown separately. |
| Other cost inclusions *(where LCC may be part of a wider economic evaluation study – i.e. whole life costs, or life cycle environmental assessment/or other)* | State:<br><br>• Any items that have been included that are outside the normal scope of LCC plans (e.g. non-construction costs, income and externalities, intangibles)<br>• Any user specific costs not in the standard forms that are included<br>• Any abnormal costs affecting the LCC plan (e.g. allowance for future legislative changes, non-adoption of roads etc.)<br>• Any specific allowances for inflation (other than that implicit in the discount rate selected). |
| Exclusions | State:<br><br>Any items in the standard form that have been excluded from the LCC. |
| Presentation of costs | State:<br><br>• How costs have been presented (e.g. discounted, net present value or other)<br>• Other financial reporting requirements (e.g. internal rate of return, capital to cost-in-use ratio, payback period etc.)<br>• Metrics – refer to Section 5 for guidance and detailed instructions. |

| LCC Descriptor | Project Information and Data Sources – (as applicable) |
|---|---|
| Discount/interest rates | State:<br>• Client requirements<br>• Discount interest rates used in the calculation (if applicable)<br>• Where discount rates are nominal (i.e. including an element of inflation). |
| Risks and uncertainty | State – LCC assessment of the risks and uncertainty with reference to the LCC risk register. Decide on what risk provision shall be included.<br>*Note – Refer to Section 6 for guidance and detailed instruction on the risks and uncertainty associated with life cycle costing and to the example life cycle costing risk log included in Annex D of this document.* |

## Additional project-specific information and data assumptions

7.4 Additional building information may be required for specific projects, which will determine the scope and how the LCCs are presented and reported. For example, public-sector schools projects require additional information, such as:

- school characteristics (e.g. pupil numbers, school type, base accommodation space areas);
- abnormal and enhancement costs expressed separately from base build costs;
- era of building to be refurbished (e.g. Victorian, post-war, 1960s–1970s, > 1980, etc.);
- new schools' configuration (e.g. levels, orientation, typical forms of accommodation layout).

## Levels of cost analysis used at different stages of design detailing

7.5 Life cycle costing can be undertaken at various levels, depending on the information available and the type of analysis used (i.e. benchmark level analysis, detailed life cycle costing based on various levels such as cost-significant key building items, construction elements down to sub-elemental and component level analysis).

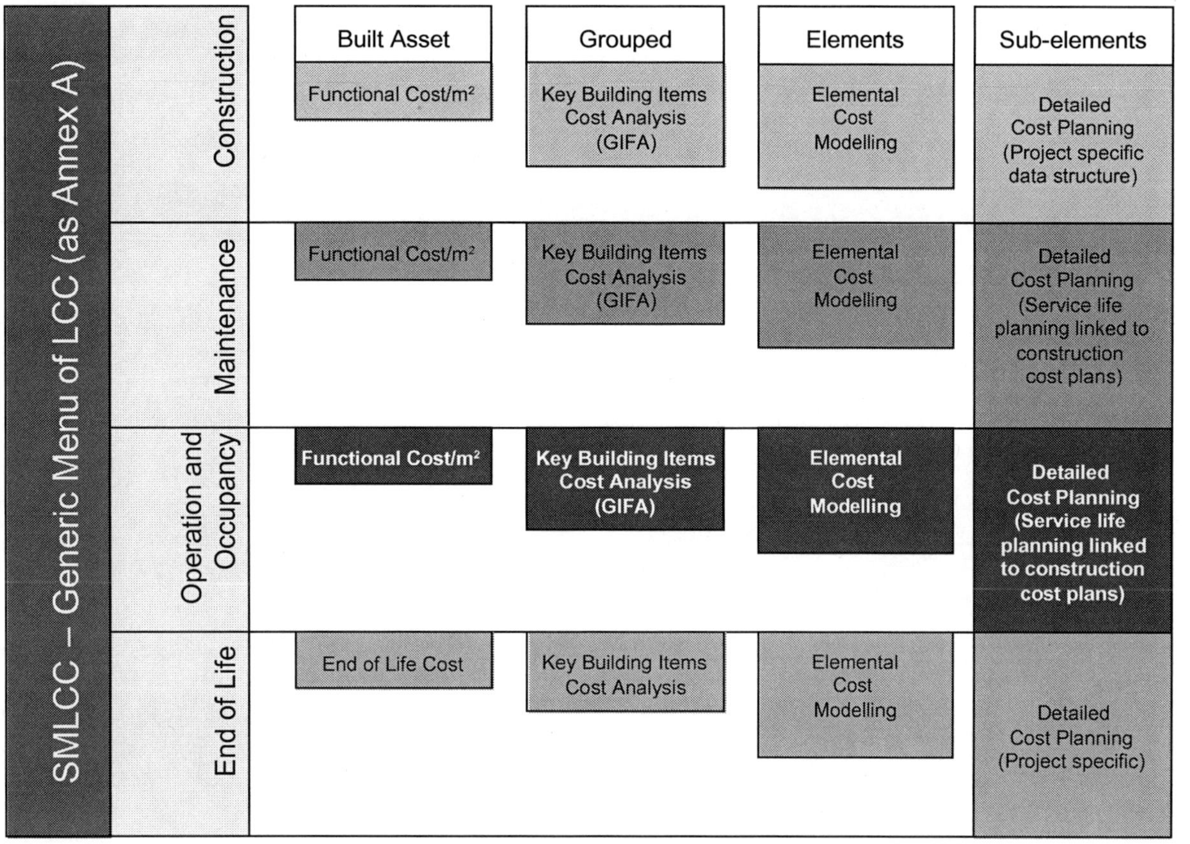


*Figure 7.1 Example of typical levels of LCC analysis, aligned to SMLCC Menu of costs.*

*(adapted from BS ISO 15686-5, Figure E.1)*

# TERMS, DEFINITIONS AND ABBREVIATIONS 8

## Reference documents

8.1 BS ISO 15686-5 provides the international standard terms, definitions and abbreviations relating to life cycle costing.

*Note: this document does not repeat all of these definitions.*

8.2 BCIS Standard Form of Cost Analysis (SFCA) provides the UK industry accepted definitions for construction (capital) cost analysis.

8.3 Annex G provides a bibliography of other reference sources of information and life cycle costing data, which include the specific terms, definitions and abbreviations.

8.4 The following glossary of terms is from the BS ISO 15686-5 for life cycle costing. For ease of reference, only key terms, definitions and abbreviations are reproduced.

## Glossary of terms, abbreviations and definitions

**Capital cost** 'Initial construction costs and the costs of initial adaptation where these are treated as capital expenditure.'

*(BS ISO 15686-5, 3.1.1.2)*

**Discounted cost** 'Resulting cost when the real cost is discounted by the real discount rate or when the nominal cost is discounted by the nominal discount rate.'

*(BS ISO 15686-5, 3.1.1.3)*

**Disposal costs** 'Costs associated with disposal of the asset at the end of its life cycle, including taking into account any asset transfer obligations'.

*(BS ISO 15686-5, 3.1.1.4)*

**End of life cost** Net cost or fee of disposing of an asset at the end of its service life or interest period, including: costs resulting from decommissioning, deconstruction and demolition of a building; recycling and making environmentally safe; recovery and disposal of components and materials; and transport and regulatory costs.

*(BS ISO 15686-5, 3.1.1.5)*

**Escalation rate** 'Positive or negative factor or rate reflecting an estimate of differential increase/decrease in the general price level for a particular commodity, or group of commodities, or resource.'

*(BS ISO 15686-5, 3.1.3.2)*

**Externality** 'Quantifiable costs or benefits that occur when the actions of organizations and individuals have an effect on people other than themselves, such as non-construction costs, income and wider social and business costs.'

*(BS ISO 15686-5, 3.1.4.2)*

**Life cycle** 'Consecutive and interlinked stages of the object under consideration.'

*(BS ISO 15686-5, 3.1.3.4)*

**Life cycle cost (LCC)** 'Cost of an asset or its parts throughout its life cycle, while fulfilling the performance requirements.'

*(BS ISO 15686-5, 3.1.1.7)*

**Life cycle costing** 'Methodology for the systematic economic evaluation of life cycle costs over a period of analysis, as defined in the agreed scope.'
*Note: life cycle costing can address a period of analysis that covers the entire life cycle or selected stage(s) or periods of interest therein.*

*(BS ISO 15686-5, 3.1.1.8)*

**Maintenance costs** 'Total of necessarily incurred labour, material and other related costs incurred to retain a building or its parts in a state in which it can perform its required function.'

*(BS ISO 15686-5, 3.1.1.9)*

**Net present value (NPV)** The sum of the discounted future cash flows. Where only costs are included, this can be termed net present cost (NPC).

*(BS ISO 15686-5, 3.1.2.1)*

**Nominal cost** 'Expected price which will be paid when a cost is due to be paid, including estimated changes in price due to, for example, forecast change in efficiency, inflation or deflation and technology.'

*(BS ISO 15686-5, 3.1.1.10)*

**Nominal discount rate** 'Factor or rate used to relate present and future money values in comparable terms taking into account the general inflation/deflation rate.'

*(BS ISO 15686-5, 3.1.3.5)*

**Operation cost** 'Costs incurred in running and managing the facility or built environment, including administration support services.'

*(BS ISO 15686-5, 3.1.1.11)*

**Period of analysis** Period of time over which LCCs or WLCs are analyzed.

*(BS ISO 15686-5, 3.1.3.6)*

**Present day value (PDV)** 'Monies accruing in the future that have been discounted to account for the fact that they are worth less at the time of calculation.'

*(BS ISO 15686-5, 3.1.2.2)*

**Real cost** 'Cost expressed as a value as at the base date, including estimated changes in price due to forecast changes in efficiency and technology, but excluding general price inflation or deflation.'

*(BS ISO 15686-5, 3.1.1.12)*

**Real discount rate** 'Factor or rate used to relate present and future money values in comparable terms, not taking into account the general or specific inflation in the cost of a particular asset under consideration.'

*(BS ISO 15686-5, 3.1.3.7)*

**Residual value** 'Value assigned to an asset at the end of the period of analysis.'

*(BS ISO 15686-5, 3.1.3.8)*

**Risk** 'Likelihood of an event or failure occurring, and the consequences, or impact, of that event or failure.'

*(BS ISO 15686-5, 3.1.4.4)*

**Sensitivity analysis** 'Test of the outcome of an analysis by altering one or more parameters from initial value(s).'

*(BS ISO 15686-5, 3.1.2.3)*

**Sunk cost** 'Costs of goods and services incurred or irrevocably committed.'
*Note: these are ignored in an appraisal. The opportunity costs of obtaining or continuing to tie up capital are however included in WLC analysis and the opportunity costs of using assets can be dealt with as costs in life cycle costing analysis.*

*(BS ISO 15686-5, 3.1.1.13)*

**Time value of money** 'Measurement of the difference between future monies and the present day value of monies.'

*(BS ISO 15686-5, 3.1.4.5)*

**Uncertainty** 'Lack of certain, deterministic values for the variable inputs used in an LCC analysis of an asset.'

*(BS ISO 15686-5, 3.1.4.6)*

**Whole life cost (WLC)** All significant and relevant initial and future costs and benefits of an asset, throughout its life cycle, while fulfilling the performance requirements.

*(BS ISO 15686-5, 3.1.14)*

**Whole-life costing** 'Methodology for the systematic economic consideration of all whole life costs and benefits (such as finance, business costs, income from land sale, user costs) over a period of analysis, as defined in the agreed scope.'

*(BS ISO 15686-5, 3.1.1.15)*

*Note: additional cost definitions commonly used in the UK construction industry are included in Section 3.*

# ANNEXES

# ANNEX A

## Menu of life cycle costs and whole life cycle costs

| | LIFE CYCLE COSTS | INCLUDE/EXCLUDE | COMMENT |
|---|---|---|---|
| 1 | Construction costs | | |
| 1.1 | Construction works costs (see Annex A2 SFCA) | | |
| 1.2 | Other construction related costs | | |
| 1.3 | Client definable costs | | |
| 2 | Maintenance costs | | |
| 2.1 | Major replacement costs | | |
| 2.2 | Subsequent refurbishment and adaptation costs | | |
| 2.3 | Redecorations | | |
| 2.4 | Minor replacement, repairs and maintenance costs | | |
| 2.5 | Unscheduled replacement, repairs and maintenance costs | | |
| 2.6 | Grounds maintenance | | |
| 2.7 | Client definable costs | | |
| 3 | Operation costs | | |
| 3.1 | Cleaning costs | | |
| 3.1.1 | Windows and external surfaces | | |
| 3.1.2 | Internal cleaning | | |
| 3.1.3 | Specialist cleaning | | |
| 3.1.4 | External works cleaning | | |
| 3.2 | Utilities costs | | |
| 3.2.1 | Fuel | | |
| 3.2.2 | Water and drainage | | |
| 3.3 | Administrative costs | | |
| 3.3.1 | Property management | | |
| 3.3.2 | Staff engaged in servicing the building | | |
| 3.3.3 | Waste management/disposal | | |
| 3.4 | Overheads costs | | |
| 3.5 | Taxes (if applicable) | | |
| 3.6 | Client definable costs | | |
| 4 | Occupancy costs | | |
| 4.1 | Internal moves (churn) | | |
| 4.2 | Reception and customer hosting | | |

| | | | |
|---|---|---|---|
| 4.3 | Security | | |
| 4.4 | Helpdesk | | |
| 4.5 | Switchboard/telephones | | |
| 4.6 | Post room – mail services/courier and external distribution services | | |
| 4.7 | ICT and IT services | | |
| 4.8 | Library services | | |
| 4.9 | Catering and hospitality | | |
| 4.10 | Laundry | | |
| 4.11 | Vending | | |
| 4.12 | Occupier's furniture, fittings and equipment (FF&E) | | |
| 4.13 | Internal plants and landscaping | | |
| 4.14 | Stationery and reprographics | | |
| 4.15 | Porters | | |
| 4.16 | Car parking charges | | |
| 4.17 | Client definable costs | | |
| 5 | End of life costs | | |
| 5.1 | Disposal inspections | | |
| 5.2 | Demolition | | |
| 5.3 | Reinstatement to meet contractual requirements | | |
| 5.4 | Client definable costs | | |
| | **WHOLE LIFE COSTS** | | |
| 6 | Non-construction costs | | |
| 6.1 | Land and enabling works | | |
| 6.2 | Finance cost | | |
| 6.3 | Rent costs | | |
| 6.4 | Strategic estate management | | |
| 6.5 | Space charges | | |
| 6.6 | Taxes on cost | | |
| 6.7 | Client definable costs | | |
| 7 | Income | | |
| 7.1 | Income from sales | | |
| 7.2 | Third party income during occupation | | |
| 7.3 | Taxes on income | | |
| 7.4 | Loss of income | | |
| 7.5 | Client definable income | | |
| 8 | Externalities | | |
| 8.1 | Client defined externalities | | |

*Note: Agree the precise scope of costs to be included or excluded by filling in (yes/no) and record any comments as applicable.*

# ANNEX B

## BCIS Standard form of cost analysis (SFCA) – UK capital cost data structure (Revised 2008)

| Group Element | Element | Sub-Element |
|---|---|---|
| **1 Substructure** | 1A Substructure | 1A1 Standard Foundations |
| | | 1A2 Special Foundations |
| | | 1A3 Lowest Floor Bed/Slab |
| | | 1A4 Basement Excavation |
| | | 1A5 Basement Retaining Walls |
| **2 Superstructure** | 2A Frame | 2A1 Frame |
| | 2B Upper Floors | 2B1 Upper Floors |
| | 2C Roof | 2C1 Roof Structure |
| | | 2C2 Roof Coverings |
| | | 2C3 Roof Drainage |
| | | 2C4 Rooflights and Openings |
| | | 2C5 Roof Features |
| | 2D Stairs | 2D1 Stair Structure |
| | | 2D2 Stair Finishes |
| | | 2D3 Stair Balustrades and Handrails |
| | 2E External Walls | 2E1 External Enclosing Walls |
| | | 2E2 External Wall Finishes |
| | | 2E3 Solar/Rain Screening |
| | | 2E4 Basement Walls |
| | | 2E5 Façade Access |
| | 2F Windows and External Doors | 2F1 External Windows |
| | | 2F2 External Doors |
| | 2G Internal Walls and Partitions | 2G1 Internal Walls/Partitions |
| | | 2G2 Balustrades and Handrails |
| | | 2G3 Moveable Room Dividers |
| | | 2G4 Cubicles |
| | 2H Internal Doors | 2H1 Internal Doors |
| **3 Finishes** | 3A Wall Finishes | 3A1 Wall Finishes |
| | 3B Floor Finishes | 3B1 Finishes to Floors |
| | | 3B2 Raised Access Floors |
| | 3C Ceiling Finishes | 3C1 Finishes to Ceilings |
| | | 3C2 Suspended Ceilings |
| **4 Fittings** | 4A Fittings and Furnishings | 4A1 Fittings, Fixtures and Furniture |
| | | 4A2 Soft Furnishing |
| | | 4A3 Works of Art |
| | | 4A4 Equipment |
| **5 Services** | 5A Sanitary Appliances | 5A1 Sanitaryware |
| | | 5A2 Pods |
| | 5B Services Equipment | 5B1 Services Equipment |
| | 5C Disposal Installations | 5C1 Internal Drainage |
| | | 5C2 Refuse Disposal |
| | | 5C3 Chemical and Industrial Liquid Waste Disposal |
| | 5D Water Installations | 5D1 Mains Supply |
| | | 5D2 Cold Water Services |
| | | 5D3 Hot Water Services |
| | | 5D4 Steam and Condensate |
| | 5E Heat Source | 5E1 Heat Source |
| | 5F Space Heating and Air Conditioning | 5F1 Central Heating |
| | | 5F2 Local Heating |
| | | 5F3 Central Cooling |

| | | |
|---|---|---|
| | | 5F4 Local Cooling<br>5F5 Central Heating and Cooling<br>5F6 Local Heating and Cooling<br>5F7 Central Air Conditioning<br>5F8 Local Air Conditioning<br>5F9 Instrumentation and Controls for More than One System |
| | 5G Ventilating System | 5G1 Central Ventilation<br>5G2 Smoke Ventilation<br>5G3 Local and Special Ventilation |
| | 5H Electrical Installations | 5H1 Electric Source and Mains<br>5H2 Electric Power Supplies<br>5H3 Electric Lighting<br>5H4 Electric Light Fittings<br>5H5 Specialist Lighting<br>5H6 Local Electricity Supply<br>5H7 Earthing Systems |
| | 5I Fuel Installations | 5I1 Fuel Installations |
| | 5J Lift and Conveyor Installations | 5J1 Lifts and Enclosed Hoists<br>5J2 Escalators<br>5J3 Conveyors<br>5J4 Dock Levellers and Scissor Lifts<br>5J5 Cranes and Unenclosed Hoists<br>5J6 Car Lifts, Turntables and the Like |
| | 5K Fire and Lightning Protection | 5K1 Automatic Fire Suppression Systems<br>5K2 Fire-fighting Installations<br>5K3 Lightning Protection |
| | 5L Communications and Security Installations | 5L1 Warning Installations<br>5L2 Visual, Audio and Data Installations<br>5L3 Security Installations |
| | 5M Special Installations | 5M1 Mechanical and Electrical Special Installations<br>5M2 Building Management Control Installations |
| | 5N Builder's Work in Connection with Services | 5N1 Builder's Work in Connection with Services |
| | 5O Management of the Commissioning of Services | 5O1 Management of the Commissioning of Services |
| **6 External Works** | 6A Site Works | 6A1 Site Preparation<br>6A2 Site Remediation and Decontamination<br>6A3 Surface Treatments<br>6A4 Site Enclosure and Division<br>6A5 Fittings and Furniture |
| | 6B Drainage | 6B1 Drainage Under the Building<br>6B2 Drainage Outside the Building<br>6B3 Ancillary Works to Drainage |
| | 6C External Services | 6C1 Service Mains<br>6C2 Site Lighting<br>6C3 Other Site Services<br>6C4 Ancillary Works to Services<br>6C5 BWIC with External Services |
| | 6D Minor Building Works | 6D1 Ancillary Buildings and Structures<br>6D2 Alterations to Existing Buildings<br>6D3 Other Buildings and Works Included in the Contract |
| | 6E Demolition and Work Outside the Site | 6E1 Demolition<br>6E2 Work Outside the Site |
| **7 Preliminaries** | 7A Preliminaries | 7A1 Contractor's Direct Costs<br>7A2 Fees Paid by the Contractor<br>7A3 Client's Specific Requirements |
| **8 Contingencies** | 8A Employer's Contingencies | 8A1 Employer's Contingencies |
| **9 Contractor's Design Fees** | 9A Contractor's Design Fees | 9A1 Contractor's Design Fees |

# ANNEX C

## Cost mapping the life cycle cost menu to ISO 15686-5 and to the international total occupancy cost (ITOC) codes

| ISO 15686-5 Scope of Costs | SMLCC Data Structure | | IPD ITOC Codes | |
|---|---|---|---|---|
| | Life Cycle Costs | | | |
| Construction | 1 | Construction costs | | |
| Construction of asset/Initial adaptation or refurbishment of the asset and temporary works | 1.1 | Construction works costs | | |
| Other (construction) and professional fees | 1.2 | Other construction related costs | | |
| Taxes (construction) | 1.3 | Client definable costs | | |
| Maintenance | 2 | Maintenance costs | | |
| Replacement of major systems and components | 2.1 | Major replacement costs | C3<br>C4<br>C5 | Internal repair and maintenance<br>M and E repair and maintenance<br>External and structural repair and maintenance |
| Adaptation or refurbishment of asset in use | 2.2 | Subsequent refurbishment and adaptation costs | B1<br>C6 | Fit out and improvement<br>Minor improvements |
| Redecoration | 2.3 | Redecorations | C3<br>C4<br>C5 | Internal repair and maintenance<br>M and E repair and maintenance<br>External and structural repair and maintenance |
| Repairs and replacement of minor components/small areas and cyclical regulatory costs | 2.4 | Minor replacement, repairs and maintenance costs | C3<br>C4<br>C5 | Internal repair and maintenance<br>M and E repair and maintenance<br>External and structural repair and maintenance |
| | 2.5 | Unscheduled replacement, repairs and maintenance | C3<br>C4<br>C5 | Internal repair and maintenance<br>M and E repair and maintenance<br>External and structural repair and maintenance |
| Grounds maintenance | 2.6 | Grounds maintenance | C13 | Grounds maintenance |
| Other (maintenance) and Taxes (maintenance) | 2.7 | Client definable costs | | |
| Operation | 3 | Operation costs | | |
| Cleaning | 3.1 | Cleaning costs | C10 | Cleaning |
| | 3.1.1 | Windows and External surfaces | C10 | Cleaning |
| | 3.1.2 | Internal cleaning | C10 | Cleaning |
| | 3.1.3 | Specialist cleaning | C10 | Cleaning |
| | 3.1.4 | External works cleaning | C10 | Cleaning |
| Utilities | 3.2 | Utilities costs | | |
| | 3.2.1 | Fuel | C15 | Energy |
| | 3.2.2 | Water and drainage | C14 | Water and sewerage |
| User support costs (3) administration | 3.3 | Administrative costs | | |
| Maintenance management | 3.3.1 | Property management | E2<br>E3 | Facilities management<br>Project management |
| | 3.3.2 | Staff engaged in servicing the building | | |
| | 3.3.3 | Waste management/disposal | C11 | Waste disposal |
| Insurance | 3.4 | Overheads costs | C2 | Insurance |
| Taxes (operation) | 3.5 | Taxes (if applicable) | A4 | Local property taxes |
| Other (operation) | 3.6 | Client definable costs | | |
| Occupancy | 4 | Occupancy costs | | |
| | 4.1 | Internal moves (churn) | C7 | Internal moves |
| | 4.2 | Reception and customer hosting | D3 | Reception services |
| | 4.3 | Security | C9 | Security |

| | | | | |
|---|---|---|---|---|
| | 4.4 | Helpdesk | E2<br>E3 | Facilities management<br>Project management |
| | 4.5 | Switchboard/telephones | D1 | Telephones |
| | 4.6 | Post room – mail services/courier and external distribution services | D4<br><br>D5 | Courier and external distribution services<br>Post room and internal distribution services |
| | 4.7 | ICT and IT services | | |
| | 4.8 | Library services | | |
| | 4.9 | Catering and hospitality | D2 | Catering |
| | 4.10 | Laundry | | |
| | 4.11 | Vending | D2 | Catering |
| | 4.12 | Occupier's furniture, fittings and equipment (FF&E) | B2 | Furniture and equipment |
| | 4.13 | Internal plants and landscaping | C12 | Internal plants and flowers |
| | 4.14 | Stationery and reprographics | D6 | Reprographics and printing |
| | 4.15 | Porters | | |
| | 4.16 | Car parking charges | A5 | Parking charges |
| | 4.17 | Client definable costs | D7<br>D8<br>D9 | Disaster recovery<br>Transport<br>Archiving |
| End of life | 5 | End of life costs | | |
| Disposal inspections | 5.1 | Disposal inspections | | |
| Disposal and Demolition | 5.2 | Demolition | | |
| Reinstatement to meet contractual requirements | 5.3 | Reinstatement to meet contractual requirements | C8 | Reinstatement |
| Other (end of life) and taxes (end of life) | 5.4 | Client definable costs | | |
| | | Whole Life Costs | | |
| Non-construction | 6 | Non-construction costs | | |
| Land and enabling works | 6.1 | Land and enabling works | A3 | Acquisition, disposal and removal |
| Finance | 6.2 | Finance cost | | |
| Rent | 6.3 | Rent costs | A1<br>A2 | Rent<br>Unitary charge |
| User support costs (1) strategic property management | 6.4 | Strategic estate management | E1 | Real estate management |
| User support costs (2) use charges | 6.5 | Space charges | A6<br>A7<br>C1 | Associated facilities<br>Occasional space<br>Consolidated services charge |
| Taxes (non-construction) | 6.6 | Taxes on costs | A3 | Acquisition, disposal and removal |
| Other (non-construction) | 6.7 | Client definable costs | | |
| Income | 7 | Income | | |
| Income from sales | 7.1 | Income from sales | | |
| Third party income during operation | 7.2 | Third party income during occupation | A1<br>A2<br>C1 | Rent<br>Unitary charge<br>Consolodated services charge |
| Taxes on income | 7.3 | Taxes on income | | |
| Disruption | 7.4 | Loss of income | | |
| Other (income) | 7.5 | Client definable income | | |
| Externalities | 8 | Externalities | | |
| | 8.1 | Client defined externalities | | |

*Footnotes:* BS ISO 15686-5 (2008) Scope of Costs
IPD ITOC Codes – OPD International Occupancy Cost Code © and database right Investment Property Databank Ltd 2004

# ANNEX D

## Worked examples

### Example 1: Budget life cycle cost plan at stage 1

| | |
|---|---|
| **Purpose** | Establishing a budget life cycle cost for a school, for a project business case. (Note – LCC is part of a wider whole life costing, for a Local Authority's project funding). |
| **Scope of life cycle cost** | LCC estimate for primary school building only.<br>Includes – construction, maintenance and operation costs included in scope<br>Excludes – external construction works costs; other construction costs; unscheduled replacement, repairs and maintenance costs; grounds maintenance costs; overheads; taxes; occupancy costs and end of life cost. |
| **Period of analysis** | 30 years |
| **Method of evaluation** | LCC estimate adjusted to base date prices (i.e. net present value, not discounted) |
| **Study input and rules** | Base date for costs – 1Q08<br>Year 0 – 1Q 2008; construction completion date 3Q 2009<br>Discount rate not required<br>No sensitivity analysis has been applied to the LCC estimate at this stage |
| **Basis of estimate** | LCC estimate – (based on industry benchmarks available from BCIS online service) |
| **Level of detail** | Outline Design Brief Stage – for a primary school of 300 pupils in London |
| **Information sources** | Capital costs: BCIS Online analyses<br>Maintenance costs: BCIS Building Running Cost Online benchmarks<br>Operation costs: BCIS Building Running Cost Online benchmarks |

*Table D.1 Budget life cycle cost plan at stage 1*

| | | | | | |
|---|---|---|---|---|---|
| | **GIFA** | 1665 $m^2$ | (a) | | |
| | **Period of analysis** | 30 yrs | (b) | | |
| **1.0** | **Construction costs** | **£/m²** | | **£** | |
| 1.1 | Building | 1250 | x (a) | 2,081,250 | (c) |
| | Fees 12.5% | | x (c) | 260,156 | |
| | *Total* | | | 2,341,406 | (d) |
| **2.0** | **Maintenance costs** | **£/m²/yr** | | | |
| 2.1 and 2.4 | Major and minor replacement, repairs and maintenance | | | | |
| 2.1a and 2.4a | Fabric maintenance | 9.40 | x (a) x (b) | 469,530 | |
| 2.1b and 2.4b | Services maintenance | 13.10 | x (a) x (b) | 654,345 | |
| 2.3 | Redecorations | 3.65 | x (a) x (b) | 182,318 | |
| | *Total* | 26.15 | | 1,306,193 | (e) |
| **3.0** | **Operation costs** | | | | |
| 3.1 | Cleaning | 15.40 | x (a) x (b) | 769,230 | |
| 3.2 | Utilities | 8.42 | x (a) x (b) | 420,579 | |
| 3.3 | Admin | 18.36 | x (a) x (b) | 917,082 | |
| | *Total* | 42.18 | | 2,106,891 | (f) |
| | ***Total Life Cycle Cost*** | | (d) + (e) + (f) | **5,754,490** | (g) |
| | ***Total LCC £/m²/yr*** | | (g) ÷ (a) ÷ (b) | **115.21** | |

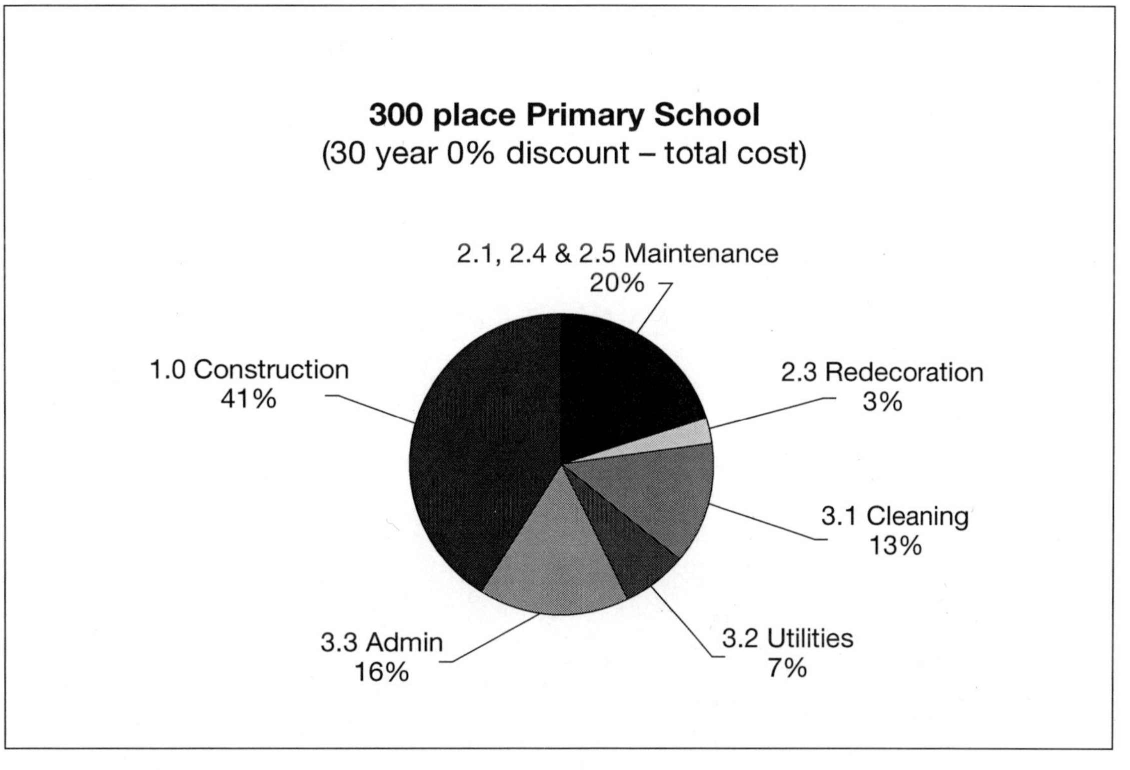


*Figure D.1 30 Year Life Cycle Cost at base date prices 1Q2008*

# Annex D: Worked examples

## Example 2: Option comparison study (with base case)

*Table D.2 Life cycle costing at whole building level at Stage 2*

| | | | | Option A | | Option B | |
|---|---|---|---|---|---|---|---|
| Project Title & Purpose - **Project Option Evaluation Worked Example** | | | | **Refurb** | | **New Build** | |
| Life Cycle Period of Analysis in years (post construction) | | | **25** | **GIFA 7000 m2** | | **GIFA 6500 m2** | |
| Base date | | | **2Q08** | | | | |
| Location (BCIS Index) | | | **London** | | | | |
| Construction Start Date | | | | **01/04/2008** | | **01/04/2008** | |
| Construction Completion Date | | | | **31/03/2009** | | **31/03/2010** | |
| Maintenance, Operation, Occupancy Start Date | | | | **01/04/2009** | | **01/04/2010** | |
| Discount rate | | | **3.50%** | | | | |
| | | | | £ | £ | £ | £ |
| Construction Costs | 1.0 | **Construction Costs (refer to footnote 1)** | | Category Costs | Initial PV Cost | Category Costs | Initial PV Costs |
| | 1.1 | Construction works costs | | 12,101,000 | | 15,254,000 | |
| | | Design Fees | | 1,900,000 | | 2,000,000 | |
| | 1.2 | Other construction related costs | | 500,000 | | 500,000 | |
| | | Infrastructure Works | | 400,000 | | 400,000 | |
| | | Planning application / permission fees | | 100,000 | | 100,000 | |
| | 1.3 | Client definable costs (In Scope) | | 250,000 | | 250,000 | |
| | E1 | BREEAM rating excellent (included in item 1.1) | | | | | |
| | E2 | Carbon dioxide emission targets (included in item 1.1) | | | | | |
| | | Construction Costs | | **12,851,000** | **12,851,000** | **16,004,000** | **16,004,000** |
| Periodic Major Replacement Costs | 2.0 | **Maintenance Costs (refer to footnote 2)** | | Category Costs | Present Value Cost | Category Costs | Present Value Cost |
| | 2.1 | Major Replacement Costs | | | | | |
| | | Generated from grouped or elemental capital cost plan - (refer to TABLE D.3 example of the life cycle replacement profile cost build up - New Build ) | | | | | |
| | | Elemental level LCR 25 yr period of analysis | | 3,900,000 | 2,477,514 | 2,842,000 | 1,687,383 |
| | 2.2 | Excluded from LCC study | | | | | |
| | | Major Replacement Costs over 25 yr period | | **3,900,000** | **2,477,514** | **2,842,000** | **1,687,383** |

| | | | Estimated Costs | Annual PV Cost | Estimated Costs | Annual PV Cost |
|---|---|---|---|---|---|---|
| Annual Maintenance, Occupancy & Operation Costs | | **Maintenance Costs (contd)** | | | | |
| | 2.3 | Redecoration - internal / external (annual) | 19,000 | 18,358 | 15,000 | 14,493 |
| | 2.4 | Minor replacement, repairs and PPM maintenance costs (annual) | 69,000 | 66,668 | 64,300 | 62,127 |
| | 2.5 | Unscheduled repairs, replacement and maintenance (annual) | 16,000 | 15,459 | 11,000 | 10,628 |
| | 2.6 | Grounds maintenance (annual) | 16,300 | 15,749 | 16,300 | 15,749 |
| | | Annualised Maintenance Costs | **120,300** | **116,234** | **106,600** | **102,997** |
| | | Annualised Maintenance Costs over 25 yr period | **2,887,200** | **1,982,736** | **2,451,800** | **1,756,940** |
| | | Total Maintenance Costs over 25 yr period | **6,787,200** | **4,460,250** | **5,293,800** | **3,444,323** |
| | | | Estimated Costs | Annual PV Cost | Estimated Costs | Annual PV Cost |
| | 3.0 | **Operation Costs (refer to footnote 2)** | | | | |
| | 3.1 | Cleaning costs | 72,000 | 69,566 | 67,200 | 64,929 |
| | 3.2 | Utilities costs (gas & elec) | 42,000 | 40,580 | 26,000 | 25,121 |
| | 3.3 | Administration costs | 26,000 | 25,121 | 26,000 | 25,121 |
| | 3.3.1 | Property management | 23,500 | 22,706 | 23,500 | 22,706 |
| | 3.3.2 | Waste management | 2,500 | 2,416 | 2,500 | 2,416 |
| | 3.4 | Overhead costs | 3,500 | 3,382 | 3,500 | 3,382 |
| | | Annualised Operation Costs | **143,500** | **138,650** | **122,700** | **118,553** |
| | | Annualised Operation Costs over 25 yr period | **3,444,000** | **2,365,110** | **2,822,100** | **2,022,294** |
| | | | Estimated Costs | Annual PV Cost | Estimated Costs | Annual PV Cost |
| | 4.0 | **Occupancy Costs (refer to footnote 2)** | | | | |
| | 4.3 | Security | 12,600 | 12,174 | 10,570 | 10,213 |
| | 4.7 | ICT and IT services | 75,000 | 72,465 | 70,000 | 67,634 |
| | 4.9 | Catering | 180,000 | 173,916 | 180,000 | 173,916 |
| | | Annualised Occupancy Costs | **267,600** | **258,555** | **260,570** | **251,763** |
| | | Annualised Occupancy Costs over 25 yr period | **6,422,400** | **4,410,477** | **5,993,110** | **4,294,612** |
| End of Life | | | Estimated Costs | Present Value Cost | Estimated Costs | Present Value Cost |
| | 5.0 | **End of Life Costs** | | | | |
| | | *Excluded from LCC Study* | | | | |
| | | Total End of Life Costs over 25 yr period | | | | |
| Whole Life | | | Estimated Costs | Present Value Cost | Estimated Costs | Present Value Cost |
| | 6.0 | **Non Construction Costs** | | | | |
| | | *Excluded from LCC study* | | | | |
| | | Total Non Construction Costs over 25 yr period | | | | |
| | | | Estimated Costs | Annual PV Cost | Estimated Costs | Annual PV Cost |
| | 7.0 | **Income** | | | | |
| | | *Excluded from LCC study* | | | | |
| | | Total Income over 25 yr period | | | | |
| | | | Estimated Costs | Annual PV Cost | Estimated Costs | Annual PV Cost |
| | 8.0 | **Externalities** | | | | |
| | | *Excluded from LCC study* | | | | |
| | | Total Externalities over 25 yr period | | | | |
| Life Cycle | | **Life Cycle Costs over 25 yr period including construction costs** | **29,504,600** | **24,086,837** | **30,113,010** | **25,765,229** |
| | | **Annual Equivalent LCC including construction costs (£/m2/annum)** | **168.60** | **137.64** | **185.31** | **158.56** |
| | | **Life Cycle Costs over 25 yr period excluding construction costs** | **16,653,600** | **11,235,837** | **14,109,010** | **9,761,229** |
| | | **Annual Equivalent LCC excluding construction costs (£/m2/annum)** | **95.16** | **64.20** | **86.82** | **60.07** |

Footnote

1 Construction costs based on base date prices

2 Annual maintenance, occupancy and operation commence after practical completion (post construction) for 25 year period

## Example 2: Supporting information

*Table D.3 Example of a capital cost build up proforma for the new build*

| ***Informative Worked Example - Supplementary Information*** | | | |
|---|---|---|---|
| ***Capital Cost Proforma for New Build - Option B*** | | | |
| | GIFA | 6500 m2 | |
| **NO** | **ELEMENT** | **New Build** | |
| | | **Total Cost £** | **£/m2** |
| **1** | **SUBSTRUCTURE** | | |
| **1** | **Group Element Total** | **500,000** | **76.92** |
| **2** | **SUPERSTRUCTURE** | | |
| 2A | Frame | 475,000 | 73.08 |
| 2B | Upper floors | 40,000 | 6.15 |
| 2C | Roof | 700,000 | 107.69 |
| 2D | Stairs | 200,000 | 30.77 |
| 2E | External Walls | 1,300,000 | 200.00 |
| 2F | Windows & External doors | 400,000 | 61.54 |
| 2G | Internal Walls and Partitions | 475,000 | 73.08 |
| 2H | Internal Doors | 150,000 | 23.08 |
| **2** | **Group Element Total** | **3,740,000** | **575.38** |
| **3** | **INTERNAL FINISHES** | | |
| 3A | Wall Finishes | 80,000 | 12.31 |
| 3B | Floor Finishes | 290,000 | 44.62 |
| 3C | Ceiling Finishes | 125,000 | 19.23 |
| **3** | **Group Element Total** | **495,000** | **76.15** |
| **4** | **BUILDING FITTINGS & FURNISHINGS** | | |
| 4A | Fixed fittings and equipment | 225,000 | 34.62 |
| **4** | **Group Element Total** | **225,000** | **34.62** |
| **5** | **SERVICES** | | |
| 5A | Sanitary Fittings | 50,000 | 7.69 |
| 5B | Services Equipment | | |
| 5C | Disposal installations | 75,000 | 11.54 |
| 5D | Water Installations | 350,000 | 53.85 |
| 5E | Heat Source | 32,000 | 4.92 |
| 5F | Space Heating and Air Treatment | 275,000 | 42.31 |
| 5G | Ventilation systems | 500,000 | 76.92 |
| 5H | Electrical Installations | 850,000 | 130.77 |
| 5I | Gas Installations | 45,000 | 6.92 |
| 5J | Lift Installations | 85,000 | 13.08 |
| 5K | Protective Installations, inc. internal CCTV | 200,000 | 30.77 |
| 5L | Communication Installations | 32,000 | 4.92 |
| 5M | Specialist Installations | 90,000 | 13.85 |
| 5N | Builders work in connection with Services | 240,000 | 36.92 |
| 5O | Builders profit and attendance on services | 120,000 | 18.46 |
| **5** | **Group Element Total** | **2,944,000** | **452.92** |
| **1 - 5** | **BUILDINGS ELEMENT TOTAL:** | **7,904,000** | **1216.00** |
| **6** | **EXTERNAL WORKS** | | |
| 6A | Site works | 500,000 | 76.92 |
| 6B | Drainage | 300,000 | 46.15 |
| 6C | External services | 50,000 | 7.69 |
| 6D | Minor building work | | |
| **6** | **Group Element Total** | **850,000** | **130.77** |
| | **CONTRACTOR'S PRELIMINARIES** | | |
| | Preliminaries | 2,200,000 | 338.46 |
| | **Group Element Total** | **2,200,000** | **338.46** |
| | **INFLATION** | | |
| | Inflation from financial close/contract award to mid-point of construction | 600,000 | 92.31 |
| | **Group Element Total** | **600,000** | **92.31** |
| | **CONSTRUCTION COSTS SUB TOTAL:** | **11,554,000** | **1777.54** |
| | **ABNORMALS & ENHANCEMENTS** | | |
| | Project specific abnormals and enhancements (client definable items) | 2,000,000 | **307.69** |
| | **Group Element Total** | **2,000,000** | **307.69** |
| | **OVERHEADS & PROFIT** | | |
| | Overheads & Profit | 1,300,000 | 200.00 |
| | **Group Element Total** | **1,300,000** | **200.00** |
| | **CONTINGENCY** | | |
| | Design & Construction contingency | 400,000 | 61.54 |
| | Risk Allowance | | |
| | **Group Element Total** | **400,000** | **61.54** |
| | **CONSTRUCTION COSTS TOTAL:** | **15,254,000** | **2346.77** |

Footnote: Specification details to be provided in accordance with the BCIS Standard form of cost analysis (SFCA) instructions. The capital cost structure used in this example is prior to the June 2008 revision of the SFCA

# Example 2: Supporting information

*Table D.4 Illustrative example of a major replacement cost profile for the new build – Option B*

***Informative Worked Example - Supplementary Information***
***Major Replacement Cost Profile for New Build - Option B***
Period of analysis 25 years
Construction period 2 years

| Year | 25 yr Total Replacement Costs (£) | 1 | 2 | 3 | 4 | 5 | 6 | 7 | 8 | 9 | 10 | 11 | 12 | 13 | 14 | 15 | 16 | 17 | 18 | 19 | 20 | 21 | 22 | 23 | 24 | 25 |
|---|---|---|---|---|---|---|---|---|---|---|---|---|---|---|---|---|---|---|---|---|---|---|---|---|---|---|
| **1 SUBSTRUCTURE** | 0 | 0 | 0 | 0 | 0 | 0 | 0 | 0 | 0 | 0 | 0 | 0 | 0 | 0 | 0 | 0 | 0 | 0 | 0 | 0 | 0 | 0 | 0 | 0 | 0 | 0 |
| **2 SUPERSTRUCTURE** | | | | | | | | | | | | | | | | | | | | | | | | | | |
| 2A Frame | 0 | 0 | 0 | 0 | 0 | 0 | 0 | 0 | 0 | 0 | 0 | 0 | 0 | 0 | 0 | 0 | 0 | 0 | 0 | 0 | 0 | 0 | 0 | 0 | 0 | 0 |
| 2B Upper floors | 0 | 0 | 0 | 0 | 0 | 0 | 0 | 0 | 0 | 0 | 0 | 0 | 0 | 0 | 0 | 0 | 0 | 0 | 0 | 0 | 0 | 0 | 0 | 0 | 0 | 0 |
| 2C Roof | 110,000 | 0 | 0 | 0 | 0 | 0 | 0 | 0 | 0 | 0 | 0 | 0 | 0 | 0 | 0 | 0 | 0 | 0 | 0 | 0 | 0 | 0 | 110,000 | 0 | 0 | 0 |
| 2D Stairs | 30,000 | 0 | 0 | 0 | 0 | 0 | 0 | 0 | 0 | 0 | 0 | 0 | 0 | 0 | 0 | 30,000 | 0 | 0 | 0 | 0 | 0 | 0 | 0 | 0 | 0 | 0 |
| 2E External Walls | 60,000 | 0 | 0 | 0 | 0 | 0 | 0 | 0 | 0 | 0 | 0 | 0 | 0 | 0 | 0 | 0 | 0 | 0 | 0 | 0 | 0 | 0 | 60,000 | 0 | 0 | 0 |
| 2F Windows & External doors | 150,000 | 0 | 0 | 0 | 0 | 0 | 0 | 0 | 0 | 0 | 0 | 0 | 0 | 0 | 0 | 0 | 25,000 | 100,000 | 25,000 | 0 | 0 | 0 | 0 | 0 | 0 | 0 |
| 2G Internal Walls and Partitions | 75,000 | 0 | 0 | 0 | 0 | 0 | 0 | 0 | 0 | 0 | 0 | 0 | 0 | 0 | 0 | 0 | 75,000 | 0 | 0 | 0 | 0 | 0 | 0 | 0 | 0 | 0 |
| 2H Internal Doors | 75,000 | 0 | 0 | 0 | 0 | 0 | 0 | 0 | 0 | 0 | 0 | 25,000 | 0 | 0 | 0 | 0 | 25,000 | 0 | 0 | 0 | 0 | 25,000 | 0 | 0 | 0 | 0 |
| **3 INTERNAL FINISHES** | | | | | | | | | | | | | | | | | | | | | | | | | | |
| 3A Wall Finishes | 54,000 | 0 | | | | | | | | | | 18,000 | | | | | | | 18,000 | | | | | | | 18,000 |
| 3B Floor Finishes | 405,000 | 0 | 0 | 0 | 0 | 0 | 0 | 0 | 125,000 | 0 | 0 | 0 | 0 | 0 | 0 | 155,000 | 0 | 0 | | 0 | 0 | 0 | 125,000 | 0 | 0 | 0 |
| 3C Ceiling Finishes | 105,000 | 0 | 0 | 0 | 0 | 0 | 0 | 0 | 0 | 0 | 0 | 0 | 35,000 | 0 | 0 | 0 | 0 | 0 | 35,000 | 0 | 0 | 0 | 0 | 0 | 35,000 | 0 |
| **4 BUILDING FITTINGS AND FURNISHINGS** | | | | | | | | | | | | | | | | | | | | | | | | | | |
| 4A Fixed fittings and equipment | 645,000 | 0 | 0 | 0 | 0 | 0 | 215,000 | 0 | 0 | 0 | 0 | 0 | 0 | 215,000 | 0 | 0 | 0 | 0 | 0 | 0 | 215,000 | 0 | 0 | 0 | 0 | 0 |
| **5 SERVICES** | | | | | | | | | | | | | | | | | | | | | | | | | | |
| 5A Sanitary Fittings | 10,500 | 0 | 0 | 0 | 0 | 0 | 0 | 0 | 0 | 0 | 0 | 0 | 3,500 | 0 | 0 | 0 | 0 | 0 | 3,500 | 0 | 0 | 0 | 0 | 0 | 3,500 | 0 |
| 5B Services Equipment | 200,000 | 0 | 0 | 0 | 0 | 0 | 0 | 0 | 0 | 0 | 100,000 | 0 | 0 | 0 | 0 | 0 | 0 | 0 | 100,000 | 0 | 0 | 0 | 0 | 0 | 0 | 0 |
| 5C Disposal installations | 0 | 0 | 0 | 0 | 0 | 0 | 0 | 0 | 0 | 0 | 0 | 0 | 0 | 0 | 0 | 0 | 0 | 0 | 0 | 0 | 0 | 0 | 0 | 0 | 0 | 0 |
| 5D Water Installations | 0 | 0 | 0 | 0 | 0 | 0 | 0 | 0 | 0 | 0 | 0 | 0 | 0 | 0 | 0 | 0 | 0 | 0 | 0 | 0 | 0 | 0 | 0 | 0 | 0 | 0 |
| 5E Heat Source | 20,000 | 0 | 0 | 0 | 0 | 0 | 0 | 0 | 0 | 0 | 0 | 0 | 0 | 0 | 0 | 0 | 0 | 0 | 20,000 | 0 | 0 | 0 | 0 | 0 | 0 | 0 |
| 5F Space Heating and Air Treatment | 60,000 | 0 | 0 | 0 | 0 | 0 | 0 | 0 | 0 | 0 | 0 | 30,000 | 0 | 0 | 0 | 0 | 0 | 0 | 0 | 0 | 0 | 0 | 30,000 | 0 | 0 | 0 |
| 5G Ventilation systems | 100,000 | 0 | 0 | 0 | 0 | 0 | 0 | 0 | 0 | 0 | 0 | 0 | 50,000 | 0 | 0 | 0 | 0 | 0 | 0 | 0 | 0 | 0 | 0 | 0 | 50,000 | 0 |
| 5H Electrical Installations | 150,000 | 0 | 0 | 0 | 0 | 0 | 0 | 0 | 0 | 0 | 75,000 | 0 | 0 | 0 | 0 | 0 | 0 | 0 | 0 | 0 | 75,000 | 0 | 0 | 0 | 0 | 0 |
| 5I Gas Installations | 0 | 0 | 0 | 0 | 0 | 0 | 0 | 0 | 0 | 0 | 0 | 0 | 0 | 0 | 0 | 0 | 0 | 0 | 0 | 0 | 0 | 0 | 0 | 0 | 0 | 0 |
| 5J Lift Installations | 30,000 | 0 | 0 | 0 | 0 | 0 | 0 | 0 | 0 | 0 | 0 | 0 | 15,000 | 0 | 0 | 0 | 0 | 0 | 0 | 0 | 0 | 0 | 0 | 0 | 15,000 | 0 |
| 5K Protective Installations, inc. Internal CCTV | 80,000 | 0 | 0 | 0 | 0 | 0 | 0 | 0 | 0 | 0 | 40,000 | 0 | 0 | 0 | 0 | 0 | 0 | 0 | 0 | 0 | 40,000 | 0 | 0 | 0 | 0 | 0 |
| 5L Communication Installations | 0 | 0 | 0 | 0 | 0 | 0 | 0 | 0 | 0 | 0 | 0 | 0 | 0 | 0 | 0 | 0 | 0 | 0 | 0 | 0 | 0 | 0 | 0 | 0 | 0 | 0 |
| 5M Specialist Installations | 0 | 0 | 0 | 0 | 0 | 0 | 0 | 0 | 0 | 0 | 0 | 0 | 0 | 0 | 0 | 0 | 0 | 0 | 0 | 0 | 0 | 0 | 0 | 0 | 0 | 0 |
| 5N Builders work in connection with Services | 0 | 0 | 0 | 0 | 0 | 0 | 0 | 0 | 0 | 0 | 0 | 0 | 0 | 0 | 0 | 0 | 0 | 0 | 0 | 0 | 0 | 0 | 0 | 0 | 0 | 0 |
| 5O Builders profit and attendance on services | 0 | 0 | 0 | 0 | 0 | 0 | 0 | 0 | 0 | 0 | 0 | 0 | 0 | 0 | 0 | 0 | 0 | 0 | 0 | 0 | 0 | 0 | 0 | 0 | 0 | 0 |
| **6 EXTERNAL WORKS** | | | | | | | | | | | | | | | | | | | | | | | | | | |
| 6A Site works | 160,000 | 0 | 0 | 0 | 0 | 0 | 0 | 0 | 0 | 0 | 0 | 0 | 80,000 | 0 | 0 | 0 | 0 | 0 | 0 | 0 | 0 | 0 | 0 | 0 | 80,000 | 0 |
| 6B Drainage | 0 | 0 | 0 | 0 | 0 | 0 | 0 | 0 | 0 | 0 | 0 | 0 | 0 | 0 | 0 | 0 | 0 | 0 | 0 | 0 | 0 | 0 | 0 | 0 | 0 | 0 |
| 6C External services | 18,000 | 0 | 0 | 0 | 0 | 0 | 0 | 0 | 0 | 0 | 0 | 9,000 | | 0 | 0 | 0 | 0 | 0 | 0 | 0 | 0 | 0 | 0 | 9,000 | | 0 |
| 6D Minor building work | 0 | 0 | 0 | 0 | 0 | 0 | 0 | 0 | 0 | 0 | 0 | 0 | 0 | 0 | 0 | 0 | 0 | 0 | 0 | 0 | 0 | 0 | 0 | 0 | 0 | 0 |
| **Total Construction Life Cycle** | 2,537,500 | 0 | 0 | 0 | 0 | 0 | 215,000 | 0 | 125,000 | 0 | 215,000 | 82,000 | 183,500 | 215,000 | 0 | 185,000 | 125,000 | 100,000 | 201,500 | 0 | 330,000 | 25,000 | 325,000 | 9,000 | 183,500 | 18,000 |
| Design & Construction contingency - Included | 76,125 | 0 | 0 | 0 | 0 | 0 | 6,450 | 0 | 3,750 | 0 | 6,450 | 2,460 | 5,505 | 6,450 | 0 | 5,550 | 3,750 | 3,000 | 6,045 | 0 | 9,900 | 750 | 9,750 | 270 | 5,505 | 540 |
| Risk allowance - Included | 101,500 | 0 | 0 | 0 | 0 | 0 | 8,600 | 0 | 5,000 | 0 | 8,600 | 3,280 | 7,340 | 8,600 | 0 | 7,400 | 5,000 | 4,000 | 8,060 | 0 | 13,200 | 1,000 | 13,000 | 360 | 7,340 | 720 |
| Management costs - Included | 0 | | | | | | | | | | | | | | | | | | | | | | | | | |
| Overhead & Profit - Included | 126,875 | 0 | 0 | 0 | 0 | 0 | 10,750 | 0 | 6,250 | 0 | 10,750 | 4,100 | 9,175 | 10,750 | 0 | 9,250 | 6,250 | 5,000 | 10,075 | 0 | 16,500 | 1,250 | 16,250 | 450 | 9,175 | 900 |
| **GRAND TOTAL: NEW BUILD** | 2,842,000 | 0 | 0 | 0 | 0 | 0 | 240,800 | 0 | 140,000 | 0 | 240,800 | 91,840 | 205,520 | 240,800 | 0 | 207,200 | 140,000 | 112,000 | 225,680 | 0 | 369,600 | 28,000 | 364,000 | 10,080 | 205,520 | 20,160 |
| Discount Factor - 3.5% | | 0.9662 | 0.9335 | 0.9019 | 0.8714 | 0.8420 | 0.8135 | 0.7860 | 0.7594 | 0.7337 | 0.7089 | 0.6849 | 0.6618 | 0.6394 | 0.6178 | 0.5969 | 0.5767 | 0.5572 | 0.5384 | 0.5202 | 0.5026 | 0.4856 | 0.4692 | 0.4533 | 0.4380 | 0.4231 |
| **Present Value - Grand Total: New Build** | 1,687,383 | 0 | 0 | 0 | 0 | 0 | 195,891 | 0 | 106,316 | 0 | 170,703 | 62,901 | 136,013 | 153,968 | 0 | 123,678 | 80,738 | 62,406 | 121,506 | 0 | 185,761 | 13,597 | 170,789 | 4,569 | 90,018 | 8,530 |

**Footnote - key assumptions and data sources to be recorded in accordance with section 4.0 and 7.0 instructions**

The capital cost structure used in this example is prior to the June 2008 revision of the SFCA

# Example 2: Supporting information

*Table D.5 Calculation of a component replacement cost build up (sample extract)*

**Calculation of a Component Replacement Cost Build Up - SAMPLE EXTRACT (without risk and sensitivity analysis)**

| Element | Component and Work Description | Quantity | Unit | Component Cost Rate £ | % of Cost or Work Rate | Quantity of Replacement | Life Expectancy | Cost per Replacement (each occurrence) |
|---|---|---|---|---|---|---|---|---|
| 2F WINDOWS & EXTERNAL DOORS | External Doors; Double; 1hr fire rated - Replacement | 138 | nr | £500 | 80% | 100% | 40 | £65,640 |
| 2F WINDOWS & EXTERNAL DOORS | Replace seals | 138 | nr | £500 | 5% | 100% | 20 | £4,103 |
| 2F WINDOWS & EXTERNAL DOORS | Replace ironmongery | 138 | nr | £500 | 15% | 50% | 20 | £6,154 |
| 2F WINDOWS & EXTERNAL DOORS | Double doors to main entrance - Replacement | 20 | nr | £300 | 80% | 100% | 20 | £5,708 |
| 2F WINDOWS & EXTERNAL DOORS | Replace seals | 20 | nr | £300 | 5% | 100% | 20 | £357 |
| 2F WINDOWS & EXTERNAL DOORS | Replace ironmongery | 20 | nr | £500 | 15% | 50% | 20 | £750 |
| 2F WINDOWS & EXTERNAL DOORS | Main entrance door arrangement - Replacement | 1 | nr | £7,500 | 80% | 100% | 20 | £7,135 |
| 2F WINDOWS & EXTERNAL DOORS | Door Controls - Replacement | 1 | nr | £7,500 | 20% | 100% | 20 | £1,784 |
| 2F WINDOWS & EXTERNAL DOORS | Aluminium; polyester powder coated; double glazed units - Replacement | 1,181 | nr | £400 | 100% | 100% | 40 | £561,748 |
| 2F WINDOWS & EXTERNAL DOORS | Replace ironmongery | 1,181 | nr | £400 | 15% | 100% | 16 | £84,262 |

Footnote - Assumptions and data sources to be recorded in accordance with section 4.0 and 7.0

*Table D.6 Cost backup proforma for FM cost for new build*

***Informative Worked Example - Supplementary Information (SAMPLE EXTRACT)***
***Cost Backup Proforma for FM Costs for New Build - Option B***

***Facilities Management Cost Forecasts***
Annualised FM Costs

| Cost Category | Management £ | Direct Staff/ Or Contracted Costs £ | Material £ | Equipment £ | Overhead & Profit £ | Risk/ Contingency £ | Total Annualised Cost £ |
|---|---|---|---|---|---|---|---|
| **Hard FM:** | | | | | | | |
| 2.4 Minor replacements, reapirs and maintenance costs | | 60,000 | 5,000 | 1,800 | 6,500 | 2,000 | 75,300 |
| 2.5 Unscheduled repairs and replacements and maintenance | | 5,000 | 4,000 | 1,000 | 1,000 | | 11,000 |
| 2.6 Grounds Maintenance | | 12,000 | 1,800 | 1,000 | 1,200 | 300 | 16,300 |
| 3.3 Administration of FM - property management | 12,000 | 5,000 | 1,400 | 2,600 | 2,000 | 500 | 23,500 |
| **Soft FM:** | | | | | | | |
| 3.1 Cleaning | | 50,000 | 2,000 | 10,000 | 4,000 | 1,200 | 67,200 |
| Waste management | | 2,000 | | | 500 | | 2,500 |
| 3.2 Utilities - gas and electric (consumption provision) | | | | | | 2,000 | 26,000 |
| 4.3 Security | | 7,000 | 700 | 2,000 | 650 | 220 | 10,570 |
| 4.7 ICT and IT services | | 48,000 | 10,000 | 2,000 | 8,000 | 2,000 | 70,000 |
| 4.9 Catering (excluding income) | 25,000 | 65,000 | 67,500 | 5,500 | 15,000 | 2,000 | 180,000 |

Footnote - Assumptions and data sources to be recorded in accordance with section 4.0 and 7.0

## Example 3

### Stage 4: Component level option appraisal example – doors

| | |
|---|---|
| **Purpose** | To compare the LCC for similar components to inform specification selection |
| **Scope of LCC** | LCC estimate for doors only.<br>Includes – construction, maintenance and operation costs<br>Excludes – occupancy costs, end of life costs, VAT. |
| **Period of analysis** | 60 years |
| **Method of evaluation** | NPV LCC comparison |
| **Study input and rules** | Base date for costs – 1Q08<br>Year 0 – 2008<br>Discount rate – 3%<br>No sensitivity analysis has been applied to the LCC estimate at this stage |
| **Basis for comparison** | LCC estimates from industry benchmarks |
| **Level of detail** | Outline Design Brief Stage for a primary school of 300 pupils in London |
| **Information sources** | Option Appraisal Format: Surveyors Handbook<br>Construction costs: industry benchmarks<br>Maintenance costs: industry benchmarks<br>Operation costs: guestimated costs<br>Component service lives: BCIS Life Expectancy of Building Components |

*Table D.7 Component level option appraisal*

| Option Reference | Option 1 | | | | | | | Option 2 | | | | | | |
|---|---|---|---|---|---|---|---|---|---|---|---|---|---|---|
| Period of Analysis | 60 years | | | | | | | 60 years | | | | | | |
| Discount Rate | 3.0% | | | | | | | 3.0% | | | | | | |
| Description | Aluminium Door and Frame | | | | | | | Hardwood Timber Door and Frame | | | | | | |
| **Construction Costs** | | | | | | | | | | | | | | |
| Capital Cost | | | | | | | £1,420 | | | | | | | £1,015 |
| **Maintenance Costs** | Capital Cost | Adjustment to Capital Cost % | Quantity Replacement % | Adjusted Maintenance Cost | Replacement Cycle (Years) | Present Value | Maintenance Cost Present Value | Capital Cost | Adjustment to Capital Cost % | Quantity Replacement % | Adjusted Maintenance Cost | Replacement cycle (Years) | Present Value | Maintenance Cost Present Value |
| **Option 1** | | | | | | | | | | | | | | |
| Replace Frame and Door | £1,420 | 110% | 100% | £1,562 | 40 | 0.3065568 | £479 | | | | | | | |
| Replace Ironmongery | £150 | 105% | 100% | £158 | 20 | 0.5536758 | £87 | | | | | | | |
| | | | | | 40 | 0.3065568 | £48 | | | | | | | |
| | | | | | 60 | 0.1697331 | £27 | | | | | | | |
| Replace Seal | £20 | 105% | 100% | £21 | 20 | 0.5536758 | £12 | | | | | | | |
| | | | | | 40 | 0.3065568 | £6 | | | | | | | |
| | | | | | 60 | 0.1697331 | £4 | | | | | | | |
| **Option 2** | | | | | | | | | | | | | | |
| Replace Frame and Door | | | | | | | | £1,015 | 110% | 100% | £1,117 | 40 | 0.3065568 | £342 |
| Painting to Doors | | | | | | | | £30 | 100% | 100% | £30 | 5 | | £156 |
| Painting to Door-frames | | | | | | | | £20 | 100% | 100% | £20 | 5 | | £104 |
| Replace Ironmongery | | | | | | | | £150 | 105% | 100% | £158 | 20 | 0.5536758 | £87 |
| | | | | | | | | | | | | 40 | 0.3065568 | £48 |
| | | | | | | | | | | | | 60 | 0.1697331 | £27 |
| Replace Seal | | | | | | | | £20 | 105% | 100% | £21 | 20 | 0.5536758 | £12 |
| | | | | | | | | | | | | 40 | 0.3065568 | £6 |
| | | | | | | | | | | | | 60 | 0.1697331 | £4 |
| **Total Maintenance Cost** | | | | | | | £663 | | | | | | | £777 |
| **Operation Costs** | | | | | | | | | | | | | | |
| Operation Cost (total £ for period of analysis) | | | | | | | £1,245 | | | | | | | £1,993 |
| **Total Life Cycle Cost NPV** | | | | | | | £3,328 | | | | | | | £3,784 |

# ANNEX E

## Example of a life cycle costing risk log

### What risks need to be considered?

There are a number of key risks that should be taken into account with life cycle costing at any stage, and the consequences and impact should always be assessed to advise the appropriate strategy for managing risk. Table E.1 presents an example of typical risks to be considered when undertaking a life cycle costing study:

*Table E.1 Example of a life cycle costing risk log*

| Risk | Consequence | Mitigation and Risk Management Technique |
|---|---|---|
| Discount rates change due to economic conditions | Investment analysis could be inaccurate | Use of sensitivity analysis to test different discount rates and related impacts |
| Design and construction risks not adequately managed, e.g. poor workmanship or design | Poor quality asset leading to defects and increased life cycle costs | Use of BS ISO 15686: part 1 'Factor Technique'<br><br>Monitoring the detailed design and construction phases<br><br>Defect management protocol in place<br><br>Standard specification based on in-use performance<br><br>Long life warranties obtained for key components/systems |
| Product failure prior to predicted life due to manufacturer defect | Increased life cycle costs, or inadequate funds available for replacement | Ensure adequate product warranties in place |
| Initial net construction prices for labour and material rates do not take account of sub-contractor costs for carrying out life cycle cost replacement works | Increased life cycle costs, or inadequate funds available for replacement | Allowance of sub-contractor 'preliminaries' on-cost element priced at appropriate market tested level on a % basis to cover site costs and mark-up (typically 8–10%) |
| Initial net construction prices for labour and material rates have not been adjusted sufficiently to take account of access costs carrying out life cycle cost works | Increased life cycle costs, or inadequate funds available for replacement | Allowances to be made for specific elemental access costs, e.g. scaffolding |

| Risk | Consequence | Mitigation and Risk Management Technique |
|---|---|---|
| Initial net construction prices for labour and material rates have not been adjusted sufficiently to take account of extra costs of carrying out LCC replacement works in an existing building and disposing of removed waste materials or components | Increased life cycle costs, or inadequate funds available for replacement | Allowances to be made for specific strip-out and disposal costs (typically 5–8%) |
| Lack of financial resources for management of life cycle costs during the operational stage | Increased life cycle costs, or inadequate funds available for replacement | Managing of a life cycle cost fund typically requires administration and management and this should be priced within the life cycle costs (typically ranging 5–8%). |
| Early failure of component | Increased life cycle costs, or inadequate funds available for replacement | Sensitivity analysis using different replacement assumptions<br><br>Risk contingency priced to cover early failure or costs of replacement exceeding estimates (typically assessed on a percentage basis, e.g. 5%)<br><br>Use of sinking fund or maintenance reserve allows for monies to be securely held in the event of replacement funds being needed at short notice (now typically a funding requirement if the project is funded privately)<br><br>Use of annual asset condition surveys to monitor performance and physical performance looking forward 5 years on a rolling basis<br><br>Detailed 5 yr life cycle forward rolling plan that takes original life cycle cost plan and adjusts predicted expenditure based on condition survey<br><br>Monitoring elemental expenditure and trends through feedback mechanism |

| Risk | Consequence | Mitigation and Risk Management Technique |
|---|---|---|
| Labour or material replacement costs higher than initial estimates | Increased life cycle costs, or inadequate funds available for replacement | Sensitivity analysis of various levels of cost increase<br><br>Risk contingency priced to cover higher costs of replacement exceeding estimates (typically 5%)<br><br>Restricting risk under contracts through use of an agreed schedule of rates with maintenance or replacement contractor<br><br>Feedback on real costs from operating projects to bids |
| Labour costs increase due to labour inflation beyond predicated levels | Increased life cycle costs, or inadequate funds available for replacement at right time | Sensitivity analysis on inflation assumptions<br><br>Price differential inflation allowance with life cycle costing (typically 1–2% pa)<br><br>Monitor differences between cost indices, e.g. BMI v TPI v RPI |
| Labour costs higher than predicted, as life cycle works cannot be carried out during normal working hours | Increased labour cost element of life cycle costing e.g. can be as high as 30% for evening works and up to 60% for weekend working | Restricting risk under contracts through agreed access and timing of work with building occupier or client<br><br>Restricting risk under contracts through use of an agreed schedule of labour rates with maintenance or replacement contractor |
| Part or sectional replacement not feasible due to poor design, obsolescence, lack of spare parts | Increased life cycle costs, or actual replacement has higher % replacement required, e.g. vinyl flooring in corridors requiring complete rather than partial replacement<br><br>Potential for mis-match of products | Monitoring the detailed design and construction phases<br><br>Supply chain management |
| Contract changes and variations not reflected in life cycle costs post construction | Increased life cycle costs, or inadequate funds available for replacement at right time | Post practical completion update to life cycle cost plan |

| Risk | Consequence | Mitigation and Risk Management Technique |
|---|---|---|
| Design expertise needed for the life cycle costing, e.g. M and E not included in initial cost rates | Increased life cycle costs and impact on time of replacement | Pricing of design risk allowance in life cycle costing for specialist items |
| Lack of availability of contractors for carrying out works | Increased life cycle costs, or inadequate funds available for replacement at right time | Supply chain management |
| Maintenance interface disputes with maintenance contractors | Increased life cycle costs, or inadequate funds available for replacement at right time as funds used for reactive maintenance rather than LCC works | Clear interface agreement or cap in place to distinguish between the life cycle costing works and reactive maintenance |

*Note: The above risks should be priced individually or as % additions to the life cycle costing. They should be discussed with the client as part of the briefing process and should be clearly stated as assumptions in life cycle costing study reports. Some of the above techniques are further illustrated in sections 6.14 – 6.26 in respect of Factors A, B and C.*

# ANNEX F

## FORMS FOR LIFE CYCLE COSTING ANALYSIS

## Form for life cycle costing analysis – 1

| **PROJECT TITLE:** | | | |
|---|---|---|---|
| Location | | Location Factor | |
| **Project Details:** | | | |
| | | | |
| | | | |
| **Purpose of Analysis:** | | | |
| Required Output | | | |
| Level of Risk Analysis: | | Scope of Costs: | |
| Owner: | | | |
| Occupier: | | | |
| Prepared By: | | | |

| **DATES** | | | | | |
|---|---|---|---|---|---|
| Plan | Preparation date: | | | Indexing Base | |
| Construction Cost | Base Date: | | | Start Date: | |
| | Date of Completion: | | | Date of Hand Over | |
| Maintenance | Start Date: | | | End Date: | |
| Operation | Start Date: | | | End Date: | |
| Occupancy | Start Date: | | | End Date: | |
| End of Life | Hand-back Date: | | | Hand-back Liability Period: | |
| Period of Analysis: | | Unit of Time: (w/m/year) | | Total Asset Life Expectancy: | |

| **BASIS OF YEARS (eg. calendar; financial year) – please state** |
|---|

| **PROCUREMENT DETAILS** | | | | |
|---|---|---|---|---|
| Procurement Route: | | | | |
| Procurement Stage: | | | | |
| Tender Basis: | | | | |
| Market Conditions: | | | | |
| | | | | |
| Tender Price Index | | Project Index: | Index Series: | Base: |
| Documents Used as Bases of Analysis | | | Source | |
| 1. | | | | |
| 2. | | | | |

*See Section 4 and Section 7 for instructions on completing this form.*

## Form for life cycle costing analysis – 2

| DETAILS OF BUILDING | | | | | |
|---|---|---|---|---|---|
| **Level of Design:** | | | | | |
| **Floor Areas** | | | **Storeys** | | |
| Basement floors: | | $m^2$ | **Percentage of gross floor area:** | | |
| Ground floor | | $m^2$ | Below ground floor | | % |
| Upper floors | | $m^2$ | Single storey construction | | % |
| Total (gross internal floor area) | | $m^2$ | Two storey construction | | % |
| Usable area | | $m^2$ | ____ storey construction | | % |
| Circulation area | | $m^2$ | ____ storey construction | | % |
| Ancillary areas | | $m^2$ | **Average storey height:** | | |
| Internal divisions | | $m^2$ | Below ground floor(s) | | m |
| Total (gross internal floor area) | | $m^2$ | Ground floor | | m |
| Spaces not enclosed: | | $m^2$ | Above ground floor(s) | | m |
| Areas Requiring Regular Cleaning | | $m^2$ | External vertical envelope (Ext. walls, windows and doors) | | $m^2$ |
| Internal cube | | $m^3$ | Area of glazing | | $m^2$ |
| Area of site | | $m^2$ | Number of units | | |

| **Function/Occupancy Use:** | | | | |
|---|---|---|---|---|
| **Functional Units** | | | **Operation** | |
| Quantity | | Unit | Hours of operation | |
| 1. | | | Peak operation points. | |
| 2. | | | Length of peaks | |
| **Accommodation and Design** | | | | |
| | | | | |

| **Building Environmental Target(s)** | | | |
|---|---|---|---|
| Scheme: | | Scheme: | |
| Target/Score: | | Target/Score: | |
| Other considerations | | | |
| **Basis of cost** | | | |
| Current price | Yes/No | | |
| Net present value | Yes/No | Discount rate | |
| Other | | | |

## Form for life cycle costing analysis – 3

| FORM FOR LIFE CYCLE COSTING ANALYSIS | | | SUMMARY | | | |
|---|---|---|---|---|---|---|
| COST CATEGORY | | | COSTS | | £/m$^2$ | |
| 1 | CONSTRUCTION | | | | | |
| | 1.1 | Construction Works | | | | |
| | 1.2 | Other Construction Costs | | | | |
| | 1.3 | Client Definable Costs | | | | |
| | | **Total Construction Costs** | | | | |
| 2 | MAINTENANCE | | | | | |
| | 2.1 | Major Replacement | | | | |
| | 2.2 | Subsequent Refurbishment and Adaptation | | | | |
| | 2.3 | Redecoration | | | | |
| | 2.4 | Minor Replacement, Repairs and Maintenance | | | | |
| | 2.5 | Unscheduled Replacement, Repairs and Maintenance | | | | |
| | 2.6 | Grounds Maintenance | | | | |
| | 2.7 | Client Definable Costs | | | | |
| | | **Total Maintenance Costs** | | | | |
| 3 | OPERATION | | | | | |
| | 3.1 | Cleaning | | | | |
| | 3.2 | Utilities | | | | |
| | 3.3 | Administration | | | | |
| | 3.4 | Overheads | | | | |
| | 3.5 | Taxes | | | | |
| | 3.6 | Client Definable Costs | | | | |
| | | **Total Operation Costs** | | | | |
| 4 | OCCUPATION | | | | | |
| | 4.17 | Client Defined | | | | |
| | | **Total Occupancy Costs** | | | | |
| 5 | END OF LIFE | | | | | |
| | 5.1 | Disposal Inspections | | | | |
| | 5.2 | Demolition | | | | |
| | 5.3 | Reinstatement and Dilapidations | | | | |
| | 5.4 | Client Definable Costs | | | | |
| | | **Total End of Life Costs** | | | | |
| **TOTAL LIFE CYCLE COST** | | | | | | |

## Form for life cycle costing analysis – 4

| | | | 1.0 Construction Costs | 2.0 Maintenance Costs | | | | | | |
|---|---|---|---|---|---|---|---|---|---|---|
| | | | | 2.1 Major Replacement | 2.2 Refurbishments Adaptation | 2.3 Redecorations | 2.4 Minor Replacement, Repairs and Maintenance | 2.5 Unscheduled Replacement, Repairs and Maintenance | 2.6 Grounds Maintenance | 2.7 Client Definable Costs |
| **1.1** | **CONTRUCTION WORKS** | | | | | | | | | |
| | **1** | **Substructure** | | | | | | | | |
| | **2** | **Superstructure** | | | | | | | | |
| | 2A | Frame | | | | | | | | |
| | 2B | Upper Floors | | | | | | | | |
| | 2C | Roof | | | | | | | | |
| | 2D | Stairs | | | | | | | | |
| | 2E | External Walls | | | | | | | | |
| | 2F | External Windows and Doors | | | | | | | | |
| | 2G | Internal Walls and Partitions | | | | | | | | |
| | 2H | Internal Doors | | | | | | | | |
| | | *Total Superstructure* | | | | | | | | |
| | **3** | **Finishes** | | | | | | | | |
| | 3A | Wall Finishes | | | | | | | | |
| | 3B | Floor Finishes | | | | | | | | |
| | 3C | Ceiling Finishes | | | | | | | | |
| | | *Total Finishes* | | | | | | | | |
| | **4** | **Fittings** | | | | | | | | |
| | **5** | **Services** | | | | | | | | |
| | 5A | Sanitary Appliances | | | | | | | | |
| | 5B | Services Equipment | | | | | | | | |
| | 5C | Disposal Installations | | | | | | | | |
| | 5D | Water Installations | | | | | | | | |
| | 5E | Heat Source | | | | | | | | |
| | 5F | Space Heating and Air Conditioning | | | | | | | | |
| | 5G | Ventilating System | | | | | | | | |
| | 5H | Electrical Installations | | | | | | | | |
| | 5I | Fuel Installations | | | | | | | | |
| | 5J | Lift and Conveyor Installations | | | | | | | | |
| | 5K | Fire and Lightning Protection | | | | | | | | |
| | 5L | Communications and Security Installations | | | | | | | | |
| | 5M | Special Installations | | | | | | | | |
| | 5N | Builder's Work in Connection | | | | | | | | |

| | | | | | | | | | | |
|---|---|---|---|---|---|---|---|---|---|---|
| | 5O | Management of the Commissioning of Services | | | | | | | | |
| | | *Total Services* | | | | | | | | |
| | | **Building Sub-Total (b/d)** | | | | | | | | |
| | **6** | **External Works** | | | | | | | | |
| | 6A | Site Works | | | | | | | | |
| | 6B | Drainage | | | | | | | | |
| | 6C | External Services | | | | | | | | |
| | 6D | Minor Building Works | | | | | | | | |
| | 6E | Demolition and Work Outside the Site | | | | | | | | |
| | | *Total External Works* | | | | | | | | |
| | **7** | **Preliminaries** | | | | | | | | |
| | **8** | **Contingencies** | | | | | | | | |
| | **9** | **Design Fees** | | | | | | | | |
| | TOTAL CONSTRUCTION WORKS | | | | | | | | | |
| 1.2 | OTHER CONSTRUCTION COSTS | | | | | | | | | |
| | **Specify cost included** | | | | | | | | | |
| | TOTAL OTHER CONSTRUCTION COSTS | | | | | | | | | |
| TOTAL COSTS | | | | | | | | | | |
| 2 | MAINTENANCE COSTS | | | | | | | | | |
| | *2.1* | *Major Replacement Costs (LCRC)* | | | | | | | | |
| | *2.2* | *Refurbishment and Adaptations* | | | | | | | | |
| | *2.3* | *Redecorations* | | | | | | | | |
| | 2.4 | Minor Replacement, Repairs and Maintenance Costs | | | | | | | | |
| | 2.5 | Unscheduled Replacement, Repairs and Maintenance Costs | | | | | | | | |
| | 2.6 | Grounds Maintenance *** | | | | | | | | |
| | 2.7 | Client Definable Costs | | | | | | | | |
| | | **Construction and Maintenance Total** | | | | | | | | |
| | | **Total** | | | | | | | | |

*Note: The costing of items 2.1 to 2.7 can be generated from either the construction costs, or elemental £/M².*

# Form for life cycle costing analysis – 5

| 3 | OPERATION COSTS | | Costs | |
|---|---|---|---|---|
| | 3.1 | **Cleaning** | | |
| | 3.1.1 | Windows and External Surfaces | | |
| | | *State:*<br>• Client requirements<br>• Standards required<br>• Working restrictions<br>• Procurement context (e.g. direct labour, outsourced)<br>• Physical environment for external cleaning e.g. availability of cradle systems etc. | | |
| | 3.1.2 | Internal Cleaning | | |
| | | *State:*<br>• Client requirements<br>• Standards required<br>• Working restrictions<br>• Procurement context (e.g. direct labour, outsourced) | | |
| | 3.1.3 | Specialist Cleaning | | |
| | | *State:*<br>• Client requirements<br>• Standards required<br>• Working restrictions<br>• Procurement context (e.g. direct labour, outsourced) | | |
| | 3.1.3 | External Works Cleaning | | |
| | | *State:*<br>• Client requirements<br>• Standards required<br>• Working restrictions<br>• Procurement context (e.g. direct labour, outsourced) | | |
| | | **Total Cleaning Cost** | | |
| | 3.2 | **Utilities Costs** | | |
| | 3.2.1 | Fuel | | |
| | | *State:*<br>• Types of fuel used<br>• Pricing context<br>• Units<br>• Details of standing charges | | |
| | 3.2.2 | Water and Drainage | | |
| | | *State:*<br>• Details | | |
| | | **Total Utilities Costs** | | |

| | | | | |
|---|---|---|---|---|
| | 3.3 | **Administrative Costs** | | |
| | 3.3.1 | Property Management | | |
| | | *State:*<br>• Details of staff included | | |
| | 3.3.2 | Staff Engaged in Servicing the Building | | |
| | | *State:*<br>• Details of staff included<br>• Allowance for consumables | | |
| | 3.3.3 | Waste Management/Disposal | | |
| | | *State:*<br>• Details | | |
| | | **Total Administrative Cost** | | |
| | 3.4 | **Overheads Costs** | | |
| | 3.4.1 | Property Insurance | | |
| | | **Total Overheads Costs** | | |
| | 3.5 | **Taxes** | | |
| | 3.5.1 | Rates and Other Local Charges | | |
| | | **Total Taxes** | | |
| | 3.6 | **Client Definable Costs** | | |
| | | *State:* | | |
| | | **Total Client Definable Costs** | | |
| | | | *TOTAL OPERATION COSTS* | |
| 4 | OCCUPANCY COSTS | | | |
| | | State:<br>• List work included | | |
| | | | *TOTAL OCCUPANCY COSTS* | |
| 5 | END OF LIFE | | | |
| | | State:<br>• Client requirements<br>• Details of dilapidation requirements<br>• Allowance for outstanding maintenance<br>• Disposal inspections<br>• Any special disposal costs<br>• Requirements for demolitions | | |
| | | | *TOTAL END OF LIFE COSTS* | |
| | | | **TOTAL** | |

## Form for life cycle costing analysis – 6

| WORK CATEGORY | | | BRIEF SPECIFICATION AND MAINTENANCE REQUIREMENTS |
|---|---|---|---|
| **1.1** | **CONSTRUCTION WORKS** | | |
| | **1** | **Substructure** | |
| | 2A | Frame | Construction: give brief specification.<br>Replacement, Repairs and Maintenance, Subsequent Refurbishment and Adaptation<br>*State:*<br>• Client requirements (e.g. meeting all legal obligations, Corporate Social Responsibility and business critical maintenance tailored to, functional failure impacts, image/reputation considerations, etc.)<br>• Standards required to be maintained (e.g. condition/performance)<br>• Working restrictions (e.g. access hours, etc.)<br>• Procurement context (e.g. direct labour, outsourced)<br>• Provision for unscheduled maintenance<br>• Insurance considerations<br>• Others – user definable |
| | 2B | Upper Floors | |
| | 2C | Roof | |
| | 2D | Stairs | |
| | 2E | External Walls | |
| | 2F | External Windows and Doors | |
| | 2G | Internal Walls and Partitions | |
| | 2H | Internal Doors | |
| | 3A | Wall Finishes | |
| | 3B | Floor Finishes | |
| | 3C | Ceiling Finishes | |
| | **4** | **Fittings** | |
| | 5A | Sanitary Appliances | |
| | 5B | Services Equipment | |
| | 5C | Disposal Installations | |

Note: Extract of form showing how to record the brief specification by element
Refer to Section 7.0 for detailed instruction on project information and data sources used to undertake the life cycle costing

# ANNEX G

# SOURCES OF INFORMATION

**G1 Sources**

This section suggests resources that could be used when carrying out a life cycle cost analysis.

G1.1 For codes of measurement and benchmark organizations, refer to:
- BCIS *Standard Form of Cost Analysis* (SFCA)
- *The CEEC Code of Measurement for Cost Planning*
- BCIS Building Running Costs BCIS Online
- BMI Occupancy Cost Plans *BMI Occupancy Costs Online*
- Total occupancy cost data *International Property Database (IPD)*

G1.2 For functional and elemental cost analysis refer to:
- *BCIS Standard Form of Cost Analysis (SFCA)*
- *Architects' Journal* and other trade publications
- historical cost analysis of previous projects
- client and consultants' cost intelligence databases

G1.3 For unit rates information refer to:
- BCIS *Building Maintenance Price Book*
- *Griffiths Complete Building Price Book*
- *RS Means' Costworks*
- Spon's, Laxton's and Wessex price books
- priced life cycle cost plans from previous projects
- specialist suppliers' quotations

G1.4 For published indices, refer to:
- Department for Business, Enterprise and Regulatory Reform indices
- Price Adjustment Formulae for Construction Contracts (NEDO) indices
- BCIS Regional Tender Price indices

Also refer to the BCIS Study of Location Factors

G1.5 For LCC data refer to:
- published data in trade journals e.g. *Building Magazine and Architects' Journal*
- BCIS Life cycle costing on *BCIS Online*
- historical cost analyses e.g. sector benchmarking (schools, hospitals etc.)
- clients' and LCC consultants' in-house cost intelligence databases

G1.6 For Service Life Data/Life Cycle Expectancies Forecasts:
- use BS ISO 15686 and BS 7543:2003
- refer to:
  - *BMI Life Expectancy of Building Components*
  - *Building Services Component Life Manual*
  - *CIBSE Guide M~: Maintenance Engineering and Management* – Chapter 13 'Economic life factors and end of economic life'
  - *BLP Construction Durability Database*
- refer to subject experts' research data
- use professional experience and judgement
- look at third party certification and product approvals (BRE and ETA etc.)
- consult manufacturers and product suppliers or specialist contractors

G1.7 For environmental assessment tools, techniques and studies refer to:
- BREEAM (Building Research Establishment Environmental Assessment Method)
- *Putting a Price on Sustainability*
- *BRE methodology for environmental profiles of construction materials, components and buildings*
- *The Green Guide: BREEAM specification*

G1.8 For maintenance data:
- use British, European and International Standards related to components
- consult services professional bodies e.g. CIBSE, HEVCA and BSRIA, CIRIA
- check industry best practice forums – public and private sector initiatives
- consult maintenance contractors and product or specialist suppliers
- use supply chain experience

## G2 A note on the use of published information

The following points should be considered carefully when using published information:
- differential rates of inflation on various aspects or elements of the building
- acute shortages in specific trades at different times
- regional variations
- market conditions e.g. energy cost rises
- basis of estimate e.g. actual tendered costs or initial estimate
- regulation changes e.g. Part L and energy performance target implications
- the form of contract and how risk has been priced for
- site specific constraints and characteristics (see item 6.18 factoring methods)
- risks and uncertainty (refer to section 6)

## G3 Related Standards

BS 7543:2003 *Guide to durability of buildings and building elements, products and components*

BS EN ISO 14040:2006 *Environmental management – Life cycle assessment – Principles and Framework*

BS EN ISO 14044:2006 *Environmental management – Life cycle assessment – Requirements and guidelines*

BS ISO 15686-1:2000 *Buildings and constructed assets – Service life planning; Part 1 – General principles*

BS ISO 15686-2:2001 *Buildings and constructed assets – Service life planning; Part 2 – Service life prediction procedures*

BS ISO 15686-3:2002 *Buildings and constructed assets – Service life planning; Part 3 – Performance audits and reviews*

BS ISO 15685-4 *Buildings and constructed assets – Service life planning; Part 4 – Data Dictionary (technical report)*

BS ISO 15686-5:2008 *Buildings and constructed assets – Service life planning; Part 5 – Life cycle costing*

BS ISO 15686-6:2004 *Buildings and constructed assets – Service life planning; Part 6 – Procedures for considering environmental impacts*

BS ISO 15686-7:2006 *Buildings and constructed assets – Service life planning; Part 7 – Performance evaluation for feedback of service life data from practice*

BS ISO 15686-8:2008 *Buildings and constructed assets – Service life planning; Part 8 – Reference service life and service life estimation* (at time of publication, due to be published 2008)

BS ISO 15686-9:200x *Buildings and constructed assets – Service life planning; Part 9 – Guide on service life declarations for building projects* (being drafted at time of publication)

BS ISO 15686-10:200x *Buildings and constructed assets – Service life planning; Part 10 – Serviceability* (being drafted at time of publication)

PAS 55-1:2003 *Asset management – Specification for the optimised management of physical infrastructure assets*

PAS 55-2:2003 *Asset management – Guidelines for the application of PAS 55-1*

## G4 Bibliography and reference material

Anderson, J and Shiers, D (2008) *The Green Guide: BREEAM specification, 4th edition*, Wiley-Blackwell (at time of publication, due to be published October 2008)

Boussabaine, A and Kirkham, R (2005) *Whole life cycle costing: risk and risk responses*, Oxford: Blackwell publishing

Boussabaine, A (2007) *Cost Planning of PFI and PPP Building Projects*, Oxford: Taylor & Francis

*Building Magazine* UK: Property and Construction Media www.building.co.uk [accessed 9 June 2008]

Building Cost Information Service (BCIS) (2006) *BMI Life Expectancy of Building Components* London: RICS

BCIS (2008) *Standard form of cost analysis: Principles, Instructions and Definitions*, London: RICS

BCIS (2008) *Building Maintenance Price Book*, London: RICS

BCIS (2007) *BCIS Wessex Comprehensive Building Price Book 2008*, UK: BCIS Wessex

Building Performance Group Ltd (2001) *Building Services Component Life Manual*, London: Blackwell Sciences Ltd

BRE Centre for Sustainable Construction, BRE Trust, and Cyril Sweett (Sustainability and Cost Consulting teams) (2005) *Putting a Price on Sustainability*, Bracknell: BRE Press

CEEC (2004) *The CEEC Code of Measurement for Cost Planning*, http://www.ceecorg.eu/pdf/ceec_code_2004_01_paper.pdf [accessed 5 June 2008]

CIB (1999) *CIB Report Publication 237: Agenda 21 on Sustainable Construction*, Rotterdam: CIB (International Council for Research and Innovation in Building and Construction)

CIB (2004) *CIB Report Publication 294: Performance Based Methods of Service Life Prediction: State of the Art Reports Part A & Part B*, Trondheim: CIB

CIBSE (2008) 'Chapter 13: Economic life factors and end of economic life', in *CIBSE Guide M: Maintenance Engineering and Management*, London: CIBSE

Constructing Excellence (2006) *Rethinking Standards in Construction*, London: Constructing Excellence

Davis Langdon Management Consulting (2007) *Life Cycle costing as a contribution to sustainable construction: towards a common methodology*, Brussels: European Commission

Davis Langdon (ed.) (2008) *Spon's Architects and Builders Price Book 2008*, UK: Taylor and Francis (at time of publication, due to be published August 2008)

Bourke, K et al (DTI) (2005) *Achieving Whole Life Value in infrastructure and buildings*, Bracknell: BRE Press

European Commission (2000) *Task Group 1 Final Report: Environmentally Friendly Construction Materials*, European Commission http://ec.europa.eu/enterprise/construction/suscon/tgs/tg1/efcmfin.htm [accessed 5 June 2008]

European Commission (2000) *Task Group 2 Final Report: Energy Efficiency in Buildings*, European Commission http://ec.europa.eu/enterprise/construction/suscon/tgs/tg2/eneffrep.htm [accessed 5 June 2008]

European Environmental Agency (1998) Environmental issue report No 6: Life Cycle Assessment (LCA) – *A Guide to approaches, experiences and information sources*, Copenhagen: European Environmental Agency

European Platform on Life Cycle Assessment http://lca.jrc.it [accessed 5 June 2008]

Flanagan, R, Kendell, A, Norman, G, and Robinson, G. D (1987) *'Life cycle costing and risk management' in Construction Management and Economics Vol 5* (pp 553 – 571) UK: Routledge

Flanagan, R, Norman, G, Meadows, J and Robinson, G. (1989) *Life Cycle Costing: theory and practice*, Oxford: Basil Blackwell Scientific Publishing

Franklin & Andrews (2008) *Griffiths Complete Building Price Book*, Norwich: Franklin & Andrews

Guinée, J. B (ed.) (2002) *Handbook on Life Cycle Assessment: Operational Guide to the ISO Standards*, Netherlands: Kluwer Academic Publishers

HM Treasury (2000) *Procurement Guidance Note No 7: Whole Life Costing*, London: Treasury Taskforce

HM Treasury (2003) *The Green Book: Appraisal and evaluation in Central Government*, London: TSO

Howard, N, Edwards, S and Anderson, J (1999) *BRE methodology for environmental profiles of construction materials, components and buildings*, Bracknell: BRE Press

Johnson, V.P (2008) *Laxton's Building Price Book 2008*, Oxford: Butterworth-Heinemann

Kelly, J and Hunter, K (2008) *A Framework for Whole Life Costings*, RICS, Scottish Chartered QS Faculty (SCQS) (at time of publication, due to be published in July 2008)

National Audit Office (NAO) (2001) *Modernising Construction*, London: National Audit Office

National Audit Office (NAO) (2005) *Improving Public Services through better Construction*, London: National Audit Office

Office of Government Commerce (OGC) (2005); *Whole life costing and cost management: Achieving Excellence in Procurement Guide (7)*, London: OGC http://www.ogc.gov.uk/documents/CP0067AEGuide7.pdf [accessed 5 June 2008]

RIBA (2007) *Outline Plan of Work 2007*, London: Royal Institution of British Architects http://www.architecture.com/Files/RIBAProfessionalServices/ClientServices/RIBA%20Outline%20Plan%20of%20Work%202007.pdf [accessed 5 June 2008]

RICS (1999) 'Part 2, Section 2: Life cycle cost planning' in *The Surveyors' Construction Handbook*, London: RICS

Stranger, C, Forum for the Future, Carillion (2003) *Sustainability Accounting in the Construction Industry*, London: CIRIA Publishing Services

Strategic Forum for Construction (2002) *Accelerating Change*, London: Rethinking Construction

*The Architects' Journal*, UK: Emap communications Ltd. www.architectsjournal.co.uk [accessed 9 June 2008]